Stories of Success:

The Young Miner
(Illustrated)

Stories of Success:

The Young Miner
(Illustrated)

Horatio Alger, Jr.

Sumner Books
Hermosa Beach, CA

TABLE OF CONTENTS

A NOTE FROM THE PUBLISHER

Once crowned "America's most influential writer," Horatio Alger is hardly known today. Those who are familiar with him think "rags to riches," and that's about it. Most young people have never heard of him.

What an opportunity!

More than a hundred years before our contemporary self-help movement, Horatio Alger paved the way with his vivid illustrations of the keys to success and happiness. Today, Sumner Books is excited to introduce a new generation of Americans to some of the most inspirational stories ever written. Regardless of your age, you simply cannot read a Horatio Alger book without coming away with a good feeling.

Alger's books initially sold in the millions and then the tens of millions and finally the hundreds of millions. In fact, the Chicago Daily News once called Horatio Alger "America's best selling author of all time." Sumner Books is committed to bringing to life this best selling collection in the form of audiobooks read by professional actors and recorded with audio engineers in our studio. Our revised e-books, each with a detailed table of contents and colored illustrations, are professionally edited, including the occasional updating of phrases to make the books as easy to read today as they were when they were first published between 1865 and 1900.

Long after his death in 1899, the magazine Publishers Weekly wrote: "To call Horatio Alger Jr. America's most influential writer may seem like an overstatement ... but ... only Benjamin Franklin meant as much to the formation of the American popular mind."

Our goal is to bring back some of the influence that Alger exerted on millions of young people in America. Yes, it's retro; it's counterintuitive and totally contrary to the cynicism that has become a part of American culture. But we are proud to be leading a movement that is as positive and uplifting as the last pages of a Horatio Alger story.

Rick Newcombe
President
Sumner Books

Stories of Success

"Always bear in mind that your own resolution to succeed is more important than any other."
Abraham Lincoln

CHAPTER I

THE GOLD-SEEKERS

A dozen men, provided with gold rocker boxes, were busily engaged in gathering and washing dirt, mingled with gold dust, on the banks of a small stream in California. It was in the early days, and this party was but one of hundreds who were scattered over the new Eldorado, seeking the shining metal which throughout the civilized world exercises a potent and irresistible sway.

I have said there were a dozen men, but this is a mistake. One of the party was a well-grown boy of sixteen with a good-humored and even handsome face. He was something more than good-humored, however. There was an expression on his face which spoke of strength and resolution and patient endurance. The readers of "The Young Adventurer" will at once recognize in our young hero Tom Nelson, the oldest son of a poor New England farmer, who, finding no prospects at home, had joined the tide of immigrants pouring from all parts of the country to the land of which so many marvelous stories were told. Tom had come to work, and, though he doubtless shared to some extent the extravagant anticipations of the great body of Eastern visitors who hoped to make a fortune in a year, he did not expect to succeed without hard toil.

His companions belonged to the same party with whom he had crossed the plains, under the leadership of Phineas Fletcher, a broad-shouldered Illinois farmer, who had his family with him. Next to Tom was Donald Ferguson, a grave Scotchman and Tom's special friend -- a man of excellent principles, thoroughly reliable, and held in high respect by all, though not possessed of popular manners. On the other side was Lawrence Peabody, a young Boston clerk, who had spent several years behind a dry goods counter. He was soft and effeminate, with no talent for "roughing it" and wholly unfitted for the hard work that he had undertaken. He was deeply disappointed in his first work at gold-hunting, having come out with the vague idea that he should pick up a big nugget within a short time that would make his fortune and enable him to go home a rich man. The practical side of gold-seeking--this washing particles of dust from the dirt of the riverbed--was in the highest degree unsatisfactory and discouraging. He was not a bad fellow, and his companions, though they laughed at him, were well disposed towards him.

Among the rest, mention may be made of John Miles, Henry Scott, and Chapman, owner of a refractory donkey named after King Solomon.

Not far away from the river were the tents occupied by the miners. There was but one house, roughly built of logs. This was occupied by Captain Fletcher and his family. He had not had the trouble of building it for he had found it ready for occupation; a previous party, who had wandered farther down the river in search of richer washings, had constructed it. In fact, it was this building in which our party had decided to remain.

"There isn't much difference in places," said Fletcher. "We may as well stay here."

"Then why was it deserted?" suggested John Miles dubiously. "That's rather strange, isn't it, captain?"

"Not necessarily, Miles. You've been on berrying parties, haven't you, when at home?"

"Many a time."

"You've noticed that many of the pickers leave good places, just from love of novelty, and wander about the field, often faring worse than if they remained where they were?"

"That's so, captain."

"Then let us give this place a try. We'll make more working steady in a medium place than wandering here, there and everywhere."

So the whole party agreed to "give the place a try."

There had been no brilliant success as yet but fair luck. In six days Tom had washed out twenty-five dollars' worth of gold dust, in spite of his awkwardness and inexperience. Others had done better, but poor Lawrence Peabody had barely five dollars' worth to show. It must be said, however, that he had not averaged more than two or three hours of real labor in every twenty-four. He spent the rest of the time wandering about aimlessly or sitting down and watching the labors of his companions, while he enlivened them by pathetic lamentations over his unfortunate position, so far away from Boston and the refining influences of civilization.

A little transcript of a conversation between Tom and himself will throw light upon the characters of both.

"This is beastly work," sighed Peabody, resting from his feet by no means arduous labors and looking over to Tom. "I tell you, it isn't fit for a gentleman."

"It is rather hard to keep one's hands clean, Mr. Peabody," said Tom, "but you mustn't think of the present. Think of the time when you will go home, your pockets full of gold."

"I don't see any prospect of it, Tom," sighed Peabody. "Here I've been hard at work for a week, and I haven't got over five dollars' worth of dust."

"I have five times as much," said Tom.

"Some people are lucky," said Peabody.

"You haven't worked like Tom," said the Scotchman plainly. "You haven't averaged over two hours a day, while Tom has worked eight or ten."

"I have worked till my back was likely to break," said the young man from Boston. "I am not accustomed to manual labor, Mr. Ferguson. My friend Tom has worked on a farm, while I have been engaged in mercantile pursuits. Oh, why did I leave Boston?!"

"I am sure I can't guess," said Ferguson dryly.

"I never expected anything like this."

"What did you expect, if I may be so bold as to inquire?"

"I thought I should find the gold in big nuggets worth thousands of dollars apiece. I was always reading in the papers about finding them. I think it's a great shame to deceive people by such stories. I don't believe there are any nuggets."

"Oh, yes, there are, but they are few and far between," said Fletcher. "A neighbor of mine found one worth three thousand dollars. Altogether he brought home five thousand dollars and invested it in a farm and sawmill. He has a good business. When he came to California he had nothing."

"That is what I should like, Captain Fletcher," said Tom. "If I could only manage to carry home five thousand dollars, I could make my father comfortable for life."

"I shouldn't be satisfied with five thousand dollars," said Peabody, whose ideas were lofty.

"How much would satisfy you?"

"About fifty thousand," said the young Bostonian, his face lighting up at the thought of so large a sum.

"And what would you do with it, if I may be so bold?" asked Ferguson.

"I would buy a nice house at the South End, furnish it handsomely, and live in style."

"I suppose you would marry?" suggested Tom smiling.

—

"I probably should," answered Peabody gravely.

"Perhaps you have already selected the lady."

"I have."

"Who is she?" asked John Miles. "Come, now, Peabody, don't be bashful."

"It is the daughter of a Boston merchant."

"Does the lady love you?"

"We understand each other," answered Peabody loftily. "She would marry me, poor as I am, but for her purse-proud, mercenary sire. It will be a happy day when, with my pockets full of gold, I enter his presence and claim his daughter's hand."

"I wish you success, Mr. Peabody," said Tom. "I hope you have no rivals."

"Yes, there is one."

"Are you not afraid of him?"

"Oh, no. He is a fellow of no style," said Peabody, drawing up his slender form and looking as stylish as a very dirty shirt, muddy boots, and a soiled suit would allow.

"I think I shall wait awhile before getting married," said Tom. "I am afraid I wouldn't stand any chance with an heiress, Mr. Peabody. Do you think I can ever be stylish?"

The Bostonian understood Tom to be in earnest and told him he thought in time, under proper training, he might become fairly stylish.

The conversation was interrupted by the ringing of a bell from the log house. Mrs. Fletcher, by an arrangement with the party, prepared their meals, and thus they fared better than most of the early pioneers. Their labor gave them a good appetite, and they were more solicitous about quantity than quality. Slow as he was at his work, there was no one who exhibited greater alacrity at meal-times, than Lawrence Peabody. At such times he was even cheerful.

CHAPTER II

MISSOURI JACK

At the end of a month the settlement had considerably increased. A large party from Missouri went to work farther up stream, and a few stray immigrants also added themselves to the miners at River Bend, for this was the name selected by Captain Fletcher for the location. The new arrivals were a rougher and more disorderly class than Fletcher and his companions. Already there was a saloon, devoted to the double purpose of gambling and drinking, and the proprietor, Missouri Jack (no one knew his last name), was doing a thriving business. Indeed his income considerably exceeded that of any one in the settlement.

Neither Tom nor any of his party contributed much to Missouri Jack's profits. In consequence, they had to bear the ill-will and sometimes open abuse of Jack and his friends.

"Come in and take a drink, stranger," called out Jack, the day after the opening of the saloon, to Captain Fletcher.

"No, thank you."

"It shan't cost you a cent."

"It would cost me my health," returned Fletcher.

"Do you mean to say I sell bad whiskey?" demanded Jack, angrily, emphasizing the inquiry by an oath.

"I don't know anything about it."

"Then what do you mean?"

"I mean that all whiskey is bad for the health," replied Fletcher.

"Oh, you're a temperance sneak!" exclaimed Missouri Jack, contemptuously.

"I am a temperance man; you may leave out the other word," calmly answered Fletcher.

"You're not a man!" exploded Jack. "A man that's afraid of whiskey is a--a--isn't half a man. He isn't fit to be a woman."

"Have it as you like," said Fletcher, unruffled. "I shall not drink to please any man. I had a younger brother--a bright, promising young man poor Ben was--who drank himself to death. He'd have been alive now but for whiskey."

"Oh, dry up your pious talk! You make me sick!" exclaimed Missouri Jack in deep disgust.

Next he accosted John Miles, who curtly declined and received in return a volley of abuse. Now Miles was a powerful man and not possessed of Fletcher's self-control. He paused and surveyed Jack with a menacing look.

"Look here, stranger," he said sharply, "just have a care how you use that tongue of yours. This is a free country, and if I choose to decline your whiskey, there's no law against it that I know of."

"You're a white-livered sneak!"

Missouri Jack did not proceed with his remarks, for John Miles, seizing him by the shoulder, tripped him up and strode away, leaving him prostrate and pouring out a volley of curses. Being a bully, and cowardly as most bullies are, he did not pursue his broad-shouldered enemy but vowed vengeance whenever a good opportunity came.

In fact, the only one of the original miners who accepted Jack's invitation was Lawrence Peabody.

"Step in, stranger, and have a drink!" said Jack, a little dubiously, having met with such poor luck heretofore.

The young Bostonian paused. He was not a drinker at home, but in his discontent and disappointment he was tempted.

"My dear sir, you are very polite," he said.

"I hope you ain't one of them temperance sneaks," said Jack, his brow clouding in anticipation of a refusal.

"I assure you I am not," Peabody hastened to say. "I have participated in convivial scenes more than once in Boston."

"I don't understand college talk," said Jack, "but if you want a glass of prime whiskey, just say the word."

"I don't care if I do," said Peabody, following his new friend into the saloon.

The draught of prime whiskey scorched his throat as he swallowed it down, but it was followed by a sense of exhilaration, and Peabody's tongue was loosened.

"You're a gentleman!" said Missouri Jack. "You ain't like them fellows you're with. They're sneaks."

"Really, you compliment me, Mr.--, what may I call your name?"

"Missouri Jack--that's the peg I hang on to."

"My dear Mr. Jack, I am glad to know you. You are really quite an accession to our settlement."

"Well, if I ain't, my saloon is. How you've managed to live so long without liquor beats me. Why, it ain't civilized."

—

"It was pretty dull," admitted Peabody.

"No life, no amusement, for all the world like a parcel of Methodists. What luck have you met with, stranger?"

"Beastly luck!" answered Peabody. "I tell you, Mr. Jack, California's a fraud. Many a time I've regretted leaving Boston, where I lived in style and moved in the first circles, for such a place as this. Positively, Mr. Jack, I feel like a tramp, and I'm afraid I look like one. If my fashionable friends could see me now, they wouldn't know me."

"I ain't got no fashionable friends, and I don't want any," growled Missouri Jack, spitting on the floor. "What I want to meet is gentlemen that ain't afraid to drink like gentlemen. I say, stranger, you'd better leave them Methodist fellers, and join our gang."

"Thank you, Mr. Jack, you're very kind, and I'll think of it," said Peabody, diplomatically. Though a little exhilarated, he was not quite blind to the character of the man with whom he was fraternizing, and he had too much real refinement to enjoy his coarseness.

"Have another drink!"

"Thank you."

Peabody drank again, this time with a friend of Jack's, a man of his own stripe, who straggled into the saloon.

"Do you play euchre?" asked Jack, producing a dirty pack of cards.

"I know little of it," said Peabody, "but I'll try a game."

"Then you and me and Bill here will have a game."

"All right," said Peabody, glad to while away the time.

A Euchre hand consisting of the five highest cards in play

"What'll you put up on your game, stranger?" asked Bill.

"You don't mean to play for money, do you?" asked Peabody, a little startled.

"Sartain I do. What's the good of playin' for nothing?"

So the young Bostonian, out of his modest pile was tempted to stake an ounce of gold dust. Though his head was hardly in a condition to follow the game intelligently, he won, or at least Bill and Jack told him he had, and for the first time Lawrence felt the rapture of the successful gambler, as he gathered in his winnings.

"He plays a steep game, Bill," said Jack.

"Tip-top. A No. 1."

"I believe I do play a pretty good game," said the flattered Peabody. "My friends in Boston used to say so."

"You're hard to beat, and no mistake," said Bill. "Try another game."

"I'm ready, gentlemen," said Peabody, with alacrity.

"It's a great deal easier earning money this way," he reflected, regarding complacently the two ounces of dust which represented his winnings, "than washing dirt out of the river." And the poor dupe congratulated himself that a new way of securing the favors of fortune had been opened to him.

The reader will easily guess that Lawrence Peabody did not win the next game, nor will he be surprised to hear that when he left the saloon his pockets were empty.

"Better luck next time, stranger," said Jack, carelessly. "Take a drink before you go?"

Peabody accepted the invitation, and soon after staggered into the tent occupied by Tom and his friend Ferguson.

"What's the matter, Mr. Peabody?" asked Tom. "Are you sick?"

"Yes," answered Peabody, sinking to the floor. "Something's the matter with my head. I don't feel well."

"Have you been to the saloon, Mr. Peabody?" asked Ferguson.

"Yes," answered the Bostonian.

"And while there you drank some of their vile whiskey, didn't you?"

"I'm a free man, Mr. Ferguson. If I choose to drink, what--what business is it--yours?"

"None, except as a friend I advise you not to go there again."

Further inquiries elicited the facts about the gambling, and Ferguson and Tom seriously remonstrated with Peabody, who, however, insisted that Mr. Jack, as he called him, was a hospitable gentleman.

The dust which Peabody had lost should have been paid to Capt. Fletcher as his share of the expenses that same evening. Of course this was now impossible. Fletcher warned him that any subsequent failure from the same cause would be followed by an exclusion from his table.

CHAPTER III

HOW TOM GOT ON

About this time Tom took account of stock. He had come out to California with the noble and praiseworthy purpose of earning money to help his father pay off the mortgage on his little farm. He was the more anxious to succeed, because two hundred dollars of the amount had been raised to defray his expenses across the continent. The mortgage, amounting now to twenty-two hundred dollars, was held by Squire Hudson, a wealthy resident of the same town, who hoped eventually to find an excuse for foreclosing the mortgage and ejecting Mr. Nelson's family. He was actuated not alone by mercenary motives but also to gratify an ancient grudge. In early life Mrs. Nelson, Tom's mother, had rejected the suit of the wealthy squire, and this insult, as he chose to characterize it, he had never forgotten or forgiven.

Had Tom been aware of the Squire's feelings towards his family, he never would have been willing to have the mortgage increased for his sake, much as he wished to go to California. But neither Tom nor his father dreamed of Squire Hudson's secret animosity, and they regarded his willingness to advance the extra two hundred dollars as an evidence of friendship.

But I have said that Tom took account of stock--in other words, ascertained how much he was worth. First, then, of the money borrowed for his trip--the original two hundred dollars--he had twenty-five dollars left over. Besides this sum, after paying all expenses he had accumulated, by hard work and strict economy, fifty dollars' worth of gold dust.

"I wish father had this money," said Tom to his tentmate, Ferguson. "I am afraid he stands in need of it."

"There may be a way to send it to him, Tom."

"I wish there were."

"There's one of our party going to San Francisco next week. He can buy a draft there,and send it to your father."

"Who is going?" asked Tom, eagerly.

"John Miles. You can trust him with the money, Tom."

"Of course I can. I'd trust John Miles with any sum."

"Who's that taking liberties with my name?" asked a manly voice, and John Miles himself stepped into the tent, bending his head as he entered.

"I hear you are going to San Francisco, John?"

"Yes, I start next week."

"Will you come back again?"

"I intend to. I am going to prospect a little and buy some things for myself and Captain Fletcher."

"Will you do me a favor?"

"Of course I will, if it isn't too large a one," answered Miles.

Tom explained what he wished, and John Miles cordially assented.

"You're a good boy, Tom," he said, "to think of your father so soon."

"I feel anxious about him," said Tom. "He raised money to send me out here, and I don't want him to suffer for it."

"That's the right way to feel, Tom. I wish I had a father and mother to look out for," said Miles, soberly, "but you're in better luck than I. Both died when I was a mere lad. How much do you want to send?"

"Seventy-five dollars."

"Have you saved up so much already?" asked Miles, in surprise.

"Part of it I had left over when I got here."

"Will you have any left?"

"No."

"Isn't it well to reserve a little, then?"

"Oh, I shall have some more soon," answered Tom, sanguine, as most boys are.

"Suppose you are sick?"

"If he is sick he shall suffer for nothing," said the Scotchman. "While I have money, Tom shall not feel the want of it."

"Thank you, Mr. Ferguson," said Tom, gratefully.

"That old fellow has a heart, after all," thought Miles, who had been disposed to look upon Ferguson ever since their first acquaintance as rather miserly.

The Scotchman was certainly frugal and counted his pennies carefully, but he was not mean and had conceived a strong affection for his young companion, whom he regarded much as a son or a nephew.

"Suppose you take the money now, John," said Tom.

13

"Shall I scribble a receipt, Tom? I am afraid my writing materials have given out."

"I don't want any receipt," said Tom. "I'll trust you without one."

"Nevertheless, lad," said the cautious Scotchman, "it may be well--"

"Yes, Tom, Mr. Ferguson is right. Of course I know that you trust me, but if anything should happen to me--any accident, I mean--the paper may be useful to you."

"Just as you like, Mr. Miles, but I don't ask it, remember that."

"Yes, I will remember it, and I don't mean to meet with any accident if I can help it. Mr. Ferguson, can you oblige me with a pipeful of tobacco? I'll join you in smoking."

Smoking was the Scotchman's solitary extravagance, not a costly one, however, as he never smoked cigars but indulged only in a democratic clay pipe.

John Miles threw himself on the ground between Tom and his Scotch friend and watched complacently the wreaths of smoke as they curled upwards.

"Tom, you ought to smoke," he said. "You don't know how much enjoyment you lose."

"Don't tempt the lad," said Ferguson. "It's a bad habit."

"You smoke yourself."

"That is true, but it isn't well for a growing boy. It can do him no good."

"I smoked before I was as old as Tom."

"So did I, but I wish I had not."

"Well, perhaps you're right, but it's a comfort when a man's tired or out of spirits."

"I am not troubled in that way," said Tom. "I mean with being out of spirits."

"Youth is a hopeful age," said the Scotchman. "When we are young we are always hoping for something good to befall us."

"And when one is older, how is it, Mr. Ferguson?"

"We fear ill more than we hope for good," he replied.

"Then I want to remain young as long as I can."

"A good wish, Tom. Some men are always young in spirit, but those that have seen the evil there is in the world find it harder to be hopeful."

"You speak as if you had had experience of the evil, Mr. Ferguson."

"So I have," answered the Scotchman slowly. Then, after a pause, "I will tell you about it; it's no secret."

"Not if it is going to pain you."

"Oh, the pain is past. It's only a matter of money, and those wounds heal."

"Only a matter of money!" said John Miles to himself. "I must have misjudged Ferguson. I thought money was all in all with him. I did not think he would speak so lightly of it."

"When I was a young man," Ferguson began, "my father died, leaving me a thousand pounds and a small annuity to my mother. With this money I felt rich, but I knew it would not support me, nor was I minded to be idle. So I began to look about me to consider what business I had best go into, when a young man, about my own age, a clerk in a mercantile house, came to me and proposed a partnership. He was to put in five hundred pounds, and contribute his knowledge of business, which was greater than mine. He was a young man of good parts and had a brisk, pleasant way with him, that made him a favorite in business circles. I thought it was a good chance and, after taking a little time for thought, agreed to his proposal. So the firm of McIntire and Ferguson was formed. We went into business, and for a time all seemed to go well. As my partner chose to keep the books, I was not so clear as I wished to be about matters, but we seemed to be prospering. One morning, however, on coming to business, I found that my partner had disappeared after possessing himself of all the money he could collect on the credit of the firm. Of course we were bankrupt, or rather I was, for he left me to bear the brunt of failure."

"Have you ever seen him since, Mr. Ferguson?"

"From that day to this--twenty years--I have never set eyes on Sandy McIntire."

"It was a mean trick to serve you, Ferguson," said Miles.

"Yes," said the Scotchman, soberly. "I minded the loss of money, but the loss of confidence was a sore thought too, after all the trust I had put in that man."

Presently Miles rose to go.

"I'll take care of your money, Tom," he said, "and do my best to get it safely to your father."

"Thank you, John."

15

As Miles left the tent, he did not observe a crouching figure on the other side of it. It was the figure of Bill Crane, a crony of Missouri Jack, in fact, the man who helped him to fleece poor Peabody of his scanty hoard.

Bill looked after Miles enviously.

"I wonder how much money he's got?" thought Bill. "I'd like some of it, for I'm bust. I must tell Jack. I don't dare to tackle him alone."

CHAPTER IV

A FOILED ROBBER

In the grand rush to the newly discovered gold fields all classes were represented. There were men of education, representatives of all the learned professions, men versed in business, and along with them adventurers and men of doubtful antecedents, graduates of prisons and penitentiaries. Bill Crane, introduced in the last chapter, belonged to the latter undesirable class. He had served a term at Sing-Sing as a housebreaker, and later another term in a Western penitentiary. He had come to California with a prejudice against honest labor and a determination to make a living by the use of the peculiar talents on which he had hitherto relied. He had spent a week at River Bend, chiefly at the saloon of Missouri Jack, whom he found a congenial spirit, and he had picked up a little money from flats like the young Bostonian, but, on the whole, he had found it an unprofitable field for the exercise of his special talents.

"I must make a raise somehow," he thought to himself, "and then I'll make tracks for some other settlement."

Precisely how to raise the fund of which he stood in need was difficult to decide. Moneyed men were not plenty at River Bend. Captain Fletcher and his party had been at work but a short time and were not likely to have collected much.

As we know, Bill Crane overheard a part of the closing conversation between Tom and John Miles. From this he learned that Miles, besides his own money, would be in charge of seventy-five dollars belonging to our young hero. It was not much, but it was something.

"If the whole doesn't come to over two hundred dollars, I can make it do," thought Crane. "It will get me out of this beastly hole and carry me to San Francisco."

John Miles slept by himself under a small tent at the northern end of the small encampment. He looked like a man who ate well and slept well, and this would be favorable to Bill Crane, who proposed to effect the robbery in the night. He had half a mind to secure the aid of Missouri Jack, but then Jack would expect to go shares in the "plunder," and there was likely to be little enough for one. So Bill decided to make the attempt alone.

In a small camp like that at River Bend, the movements and plans of each individual were generally known. So it was generally understood that John Miles intended to start on Thursday for the city.

The previous evening he spent with Tom and Ferguson, with whom he was more intimate than any others of the party. He would not have been drawn to the Scotchman, but for his being Tom's roommate. Through him he came to appreciate and respect the Scot's sterling virtues and to overlook his dry, phlegmatic manner.

"I hope you'll have good luck, Mr. Miles," said Tom.

"Thank you, my boy."

"I would join with my young friend Tom," said Ferguson, "if I were quite clear in my mind whether good luck is the right term to use."

"Don't you think some men are luckier than others, Mr. Ferguson?" asked Tom.

"Some men are more successful, doubtless, but what we call good luck, generally comes from greater industry, good judgment, and, above all, the prompt use of opportunities."

"There is something in that," said Miles, "but when two men work side by side with equal industry and one finds a nugget worth thousands of dollars while the other plods along at a few dollars a day, isn't there some luck there?"

"It may be so," said the Scotchman, cautiously, "but such cases are exceptional."

"So one boy is born to an inheritance of wealth and another to an inheritance of hard work. Isn't there any luck there?"

"The luck may be on the side of the poor boy," was the reply. "He is further removed from temptation."

John Miles laughed.

"Well, at any rate, it seems you believe in luck after all. I am sure you both wish me to be prosperous, whether you call it luck or by some other name. Tom, if I meet with any good opening that I think will suit you, I shall write you. You don't want to stay here, particularly?"

"No, the place is not so pleasant since these new people have come here. Missouri Jack isn't a neighbor that I like."

"He is exerting a bad influence," said Ferguson. "I am afraid Peabody visits him too often for his own good."

"He ought to have stayed in Boston," said Miles. "He is not the man for such a life as ours. He is too delicate to work, or thinks he is, and I see no other reliable road to success."

"I saw Peabody reeling out of the saloon this afternoon," said Tom. "I asked him if he considered it 'high-toned' to drink in a saloon, as that is the word he is always using, but he said it didn't make much difference out here, where he wasn't known."

"Peabody isn't overstocked with brains, though he does come from Boston," said Miles.

Ten o'clock came, and Miles rose to go.

"I must have a good night's rest," he said, "for tomorrow night must see me many miles on my road. Tom, I will attend to that commission of yours just as soon as I have the opportunity."

"Thank you, Mr. Miles."

John Miles walked slowly toward his tent. Arrived there, he threw himself down on his rude couch, and in less than fifteen minutes, he was sound asleep. He had done his usual day's work and made some preparations for his journey besides, and these made slumber sweet and refreshing.

Before settling himself for the night, however, Miles carefully deposited a bag of gold dust under his head, wrapped up in an extra pair of pantaloons. Had he known that Bill Crane had formed a plan to rob him that very night, he would have taken extra precautions, but he was not inclined to be suspicious or to anticipate danger.

Perhaps an hour later, Tom, who found himself unusually restless, got up from his hard couch, leaving Ferguson fast asleep, and went out into the air thinking that a walk would do him good and dispose him to sleep. The night was dark, but not wholly so. There was no moon, but a few stars were shining, and as his eyes became accustomed to the faint light, he could easily distinguish objects at the distance of a few rods.

Tom's thoughts reverted to his humble home, more than three thousand miles away. Probably the fact that he had committed to John Miles a sum of money to send to his father had turned his thoughts in that direction.

"Father will be glad to get the seventy-five dollars," thought Tom, "and I am sure he will need it. I wish it could get there more quickly, but it is a long way off."

Tom was not homesick and was far from wishing himself back, with his object in coming yet unaccomplished, but it did occur to him, that he would like to see his father and mother, and brothers and sisters, if only for a few minutes.

When he came out he had no particular direction in mind in which he wished to walk, but chance directed his steps toward the tent of his friend, John Miles.

When he came near it, his attention was arrested by the sight of a crouching figure which appeared to be entering the tent. His first thought was, that Miles, like himself, had got up from his couch and was just returning. He was on the point of calling out "John," when a sudden doubt and suspicion silenced him.

"Might not it be a robber?"

Tom was determined to find out. He crept nearer, so that he could have a clearer view of the figure.

"It's Bill Crane!" he said to himself, with sudden recognition. "What's he up to?"

Tom could guess. He didn't know the man's antecedents, but he had read his character aright. He was instantly on the alert. Crane evidently was on a thief's errand and was likely to steal not only Miles's money but Tom's. Our hero was alive to the emergency and resolved to foil him. He had his revolver with him, for in the unsettled state of society with no one to enforce the laws, and indeed no laws to enforce, it was the custom for all men to go armed.

Tom was not long left in doubt as to Crane's intentions. He saw him cautiously pulling at something in the tent and felt sure that it was the bag of treasure. He decided that the time had come to act.

"Put that back," he exclaimed in a boyish, but clear, commanding tone.

Bill Crane turned suddenly, panic-stricken.

He saw Tom standing a few feet from him, with a revolver in his hand.

All was not lost. He might, he thought, intimidate the boy.

"Mind your business, you young cub," he growled.

"What are you about?" demanded Tom.

"I am going to sleep with Miles. He invited me. Does that satisfy you?"

"No, it doesn't, for I know that it's a lie. You are here to rob him."

"You'd better not insult me, boy, or I'll have your life."

"Get up this instant and leave the tent, or I'll fire," said Tom resolutely.

"A young cub like you can't frighten me. That shooting iron of yours isn't loaded," said Bill Crane, rather uneasily.

"It'll be rather a bad thing for you to take the risk," said Tom, with a coolness that surprised himself, for the situation was a strange one for a boy brought up in a quiet New England farming town.

"What do you want of me?" growled the desperado, uncomfortably, for he was satisfied that the weapon was loaded, and Tom looked as if he would shoot.

"I want you to leave that tent at once," said Tom.

"Suppose I don't."

"Then I shall fire at you."

"And be hung for attempted murder."

"I think I could explain it," said our hero. "You know very well what will happen to you if you are caught."

Bill Crane did know. Hanging was the penalty for theft in the early days of California, and he had no desire to swing from the branch of a tree.

"You're a young fool!" he said roughly, as he rose from his stooping posture. "I wanted to ask Miles to do a little commission for me in Frisco. I had no thought of robbing him."

"You can see him in the morning about it," said Tom resolutely.

"I'll be even with you for this," said the foiled thief, as he sullenly obeyed the boy, half ashamed to do so.

Tom went back to his tent, aroused Ferguson, and the two took turns in guarding the tent of Miles during the night. Tom did not wish to awaken him, for he needed rest on the eve of a long and fatiguing journey.

CHAPTER V

MILES SETS OUT ON HIS JOURNEY

When Miles woke up in the morning he found Tom beside him.

"Hallo, Tom!" he said, in some surprise. "This is an early call."

"I have been here half the night," said Tom, quietly.

"How is that?"

"I was afraid you would be robbed."

"Did you have any particular reason for fearing it?" asked Miles, quickly.

Thereupon Tom described his chance visit of the evening before and what he saw. As might have been expected, John Miles was indignant.

"The miserable sneak! I'd like to wring his neck," he exclaimed. "Did you say he had his hand upon the bag of gold dust, Tom?"

"Yes; I distinctly saw him attempting to draw it out from under your head."

"If the boys knew of this, Crane's fate would be sealed. A thief in a mining camp has a short shrift."

"You mean he would be hung?" asked Tom, in surprise.

"Yes, he would grace a limb of yonder tree, and I am not sure but it would be the best way to dispose of him."

Tom shuddered.

"It would be a terrible fate," he said. "I should like to see him punished, but I don't want him hanged."

"Then you will have to keep your mouth shut. Once the boys get hold of what happened, nothing will save him."

"Then I shall keep it to myself."

"I will see Crane, and let him understand that I am aware of the attempt he made," said Miles.

After breakfast he came upon Crane within a few rods of Missouri Jack's saloon.

"Look here, Bill Crane," said Miles, "I've got something to say to you."

"What is it?" returned Crane, sullenly, looking ill at ease.

"I understand you favored me with a visit, last night."

"Who told you so?"

"Tom Nelson."

"The young cub had better mind his own business," growled Crane, in a menacing tone.

"He did me a service in preventing your intended theft."

"If he says I meant to rob you, he lies!"

"Nevertheless, if he should make public what he saw, the boys would be likely to believe him rather than you," said Miles, significantly.

"Is he going to tell?" asked Crane, nervously.

"He has told me but is not likely to speak of it to others, being unwilling that you should suffer the punishment you deserve."

"He is very kind," sneered Bill Crane, but he felt very much relieved.

"You probably owe your life to his kindness," said Miles, quietly. "He tells me you wish me to do something for you in Frisco."

"I've changed my mind," said Crane, abruptly. "I may go there myself, soon."

Miles smiled.

"I thought it might be something urgent," he said, "since it led you to come to my tent at midnight."

"I thought you would be starting away early this morning."

"Well thought of, Bill Crane, but it is only fair to tell you that I don't believe a word you say. I have one thing to say to you before I go, and you had better bear it in mind. If you harm a hair of Tom Nelson's head, and I believe you quite capable of it, I will never rest till I have found you out and punished you for it."

"I am not afraid of you, John Miles," retorted Crane, but he looked uncomfortable.

"You will have cause to be, if you injure Tom."

Miles walked off, leaving behind him a bitter enemy.

"I hate him--him and the boy too!" muttered Bill Crane. "If I dared, I would put my mark on him before he leaves the camp."

But Crane did not dare. He knew that he was in a very critical position. His safety depended on the silence of two persons--one of whom would soon be gone. He was not aware that Ferguson also knew of his attempted crime, or the danger would have seemed greater. However much he thirsted for vengeance, it would not do to gratify it now. He must bide his time.

Bill Crane was cunning as well as malignant. He decided to quiet Tom's suspicions if he could, and ensure his continued silence, by an affectation of friendliness. He waited till he saw our hero washing dust beyond earshot of any listeners and strolled up to him.

"How are you getting on, Tom?" he asked, with an appearance of friendliness.

Tom looked up quickly. Considering all that had happened, he was somewhat struck by Crane's effrontery.

"Fairly well," he answered coldly.

"Shan't I relieve you a few minutes?" proposed Crane.

"No, thank you."

"It's pretty hard work and don't pay as well as it might. I think California's a humbug, for my part."

"Have you tried washing for gold?" asked Tom. "I haven't seen you at work."

"Not here. I've tried it elsewhere, but it's slow."

"Then, why do you stay here?" asked Tom, naturally.

Crane shrugged his shoulders.

"Because I haven't money to get away," he said. "I'm waiting for something to turn up. If I could only get to Frisco, I would go into some business. I would like to have gone with Miles."

"Was that what you were going to propose to him, last night?" asked Tom, dryly.

"Yes, I wanted to speak to him on that subject. I had a great mind to ask him to lend me a little money and take me along with him. I would have arranged to pay him soon after we reached Frisco."

Tom knew that the fellow was lying and remained silent.

"You made a little mistake about my intentions," continued Bill Crane, smoothly, "but perhaps it was natural under the circumstances."

Tom thought it was, but still preserved silence, much to Crane's discomfiture.

Bill Crane eyed him sharply and saw his incredulity, but for that he cared little, if only he could secure his silence.

"I think you will see that it isn't fair to me to speak of this matter," he continued.

"I had made up my mind not to speak of it," said Tom. "I don't want to get you into trouble."

"Good morning, Mr. Crane," said Lawrence Peabody, who had just come up.

"Good morning, Peabody. I was watching our friend Tom. How are you getting on?"

"I haven't done anything yet today. It's dirty work. I don't think it's fit for a gentleman. Tom, there, is used to work, and he don't mind."

"Shall we go round to Jack's?"

"All right!"

And the two walked away together.

"I am sorry Peabody doesn't keep better company," Tom said to himself. "Bill Crane won't do him any good."

CHAPTER VI

ROBBED IN HIS SLEEP

Tom was right in concluding that Bill Crane's influence over Peabody was anything but good. The young Bostonian, however, was not long subjected to it. During the night following John Miles's departure, the little settlement at River Bend was called upon to deplore the loss of an eminent member.

In brief, somewhere between midnight and dawn Mr. William Crane took his departure, without the ceremony of leave-taking. Had he gone alone no one perhaps would have felt any violent sorrow, but he took with him a horse belonging to Adam Dietrich, an industrious young German, who had only recently arrived. No one had seen the two go together, but it was only natural to suppose that Crane had spirited away the horse.

Dietrich borrowed a horse, and, accompanied by a friend, set out in search of the thief, but returned at night unsuccessful. Had it been wet weather, it might have been possible to track the fugitive, but it was very dry, and the trail was soon lost. It was almost impossible to tell what direction Crane would choose and continued pursuit would not pay, so Adam sadly returned to his work.

Little doubt was entertained among the miners that Crane was responsible for the loss of the horse. Had he been caught, there would have been small chance for him, so generally was he pronounced guilty. A few of his companions, especially Missouri Jack, defended him.

"Bill Crane wouldn't steal a horse any more than I would," said Jack, and there were those who agreed with him without acquitting Bill. "Bill ain't no saint, but he ain't a thief."

Whether Jack believed what he said is doubtful. Crane needed a different advocate to clear him from suspicion.

It may as well be stated that Crane did steal the horse. He had a decided objection to walking as long as he could ride and, having no animal of his own, annexed the property of his neighbor.

He had two motives which influenced him to leave the settlement. First, he was in Tom's power, and he was by no means certain that our hero would keep silence touching his night attempt at robbery. In the second place, he still coveted the bag of gold dust which John Miles carried away with him. He had been prevented from taking it, but, as Miles was travelling alone, he foresaw a better chance of success if he should follow on his track.

How or under what circumstances he should make the new attempt he left to be decided later. The first thing, obviously, was to overtake him.

Crane experienced the same difficulty in tracking Miles that had led to the failure of his own pursuers. It was only on the fifth day, that, as he halted his steed on the hillside and cast long glances about him, he caught sight, a mile away, of the object of his pursuit. He could not mistake the sturdy, broad-shouldered figure and large, massive head.

"That's Miles, sure enough!" he exclaimed, joyfully. "I thought I had missed him, but I'm in luck. That bag must be mine."

The most direct course was to ride up in the fashion of a highwayman and demand the bag. But Crane did not mean to proceed in this fashion. Physically, though not a weak man, he was not a match for Miles, and he knew it. Cunning must supply the place of strength. He knew that Miles was a sound sleeper, and could think of no better plan than repeating the visit he had made in camp. It was already late in the afternoon when he caught sight of the sturdy miner. It was his policy now to keep him in sight, but not to approach near enough for recognition. Once seen, Miles would be on his guard, and the game would be spoiled. Crane halted, therefore, and drew back within the shadow of the trees, henceforth advancing cautiously.

John Miles did not once turn back. Had he done so, it is quite possible that he might have caught a glimpse of his pursuer. He had travelled since morning, and his faithful horse was beginning to show signs of fatigue.

"You are tired, my poor Dick," he said kindly, stroking the horse. "You deserve supper and rest, and you shall have it."

Dick appeared to understand what his rider said, for he gave a short neigh of satisfaction.

John Miles looked around him. Just ahead was a large tree, under whose broad branches it would be pleasant to recline. Not far away was a slender mountain stream trickling over the rocks. Nothing could have been better.

Miles slid from his horse and made preparations to encamp for the night, first leading his faithful steed to the stream, where he quenched his thirst. Then he brought out his slender stock of provisions and partook of supper.

"It's pleasant to rest after a long day's ride," soliloquized Miles. "I must have made forty miles today. I could easily have gone farther, had it been on the prairies at home, but these mountain roads are hard upon man and beast."

The Beale's Cut at Fremont Pass in Southern California show steep, mountainous roads.

After supper Miles threw himself upon the ground, and his mind became busy with his plans and prospects.

"I shall reach Frisco in three days, according to my calculations," he reflected, "and then, first of all, I must attend to Tom's commission. That's a good boy, Tom. I wish he were here with me tonight. Why didn't I urge him to come with me? He is not doing very well where he is, and there are plenty of chances for a smart boy in the city. If I find any opening for him, I will send for him. I don't know what gives me such an interest in that boy, but I'd sooner do him a good turn than any man I know. I hope that thief Crane won't play any trick upon him. If he does, I swear I'll get even with him."

John Miles little suspected that he himself stood in more peril from the man he denounced than our hero. Had he known that Bill Crane was lurking in the vicinity, he would scarcely have courted slumber so fearlessly.

Physical fatigue and the stillness of outward nature speedily brought on a feeling of drowsiness that was not long in bringing sleep. Twilight had hardly given place to night when our traveller had become "to dumb forgetfulness a prey."

This was what Bill Crane had been waiting for. He rightly calculated that Miles would soon be asleep. He inferred this from his own feelings. He, too, had travelled many miles, and felt drowsy, but, with the object he had in view near accomplishment, he was able to resist the promptings of nature.

Crane rode till he was but a few rods from Miles, then dismounted and tethered his horse. With stealthy step he approached the sleeper. With satisfaction he regarded the upturned face of the man whom, if waking he would have feared, and noted his deep, regular breathing.

"You wouldn't sleep so sound, John Miles," he said to himself, "if you knew I was standing over you. How easily I could put a bullet into you! But then I wouldn't have the satisfaction of anticipating your disappointment when you wake up and find your treasure gone! No, you may live. I have no use for your life, that is, if you don't wake up. In that case, I may have to kill you."

The bag of gold dust lay under the head of Miles. He knew of no better place for it, calculating that any attempt at removal would arouse him. So it might under ordinary circumstances, but unusual fatigue made him sleep like a log. Bill Crane kneeled down, and by delicate manipulation succeeded in drawing the bag from beneath the sleeper's head. Lest the removal of the pillow might awaken Miles, he replaced it by a coat, which he folded up so as to produce about the same elevation above the ground.

The transfer was made, without in the least interfering with the slumbers of the tired traveller.

Bill Crane rose to his feet, triumphant. Not only was he possessed of a sum of which he stood sorely in need, but he had the satisfaction of outwitting his adversary. Moreover, he had obtained

---

29

Tom's money in addition, and thus revenged himself upon the boy who had once thwarted him.

"Goodbye, John Miles!" he said, lifting his hat mockingly. "Sorry to inconvenience you, but can't help it. A long sleep, and pleasant dreams!"

Thus speaking, he turned away, unconscious that he had been observed by a third party.

CHAPTER VII

THE HEATHEN CHINEE

This third party belonged to that peculiar race immortalized by Bret Harte. He was a heathen Chinee! His face was smooth and bland, and wore an expression of childlike innocence which was well calculated to deceive. Ah Sin possessed the usual craft of his countrymen, and understood very well how to advance his worldly fortunes. He belonged to the advance guard of immigrants from the Central Flowery Kingdom and with a companion, Ah Jim, was engaged in mining in the immediate neighborhood. His gains had not been great thus far, but then his expenses had amounted to little or nothing. He and his friend had brought two bags of rice from San Francisco, and they were well satisfied with this solitary article of diet.

Ah Sin, from a distance, had seen John Miles encamp for the night and, impelled by curiosity or a more questionable motive, had approached to take a view of the stranger. Before reaching him he caught sight of Bill Crane, and his almond eyes straightway watched the movements of that gentleman, while he himself kept sufficiently in the background to escape observation.

When he saw Crane stealthily remove the bag from under the sleeper's head, he became very much interested and a bland smile overspread his face, while his cue vibrated gently with approval.

"'Melican man very smart," he murmured to himself. "He steal his friend's money while he sleep."

My readers are probably aware that our Mongolian visitors find a difficulty in pronouncing the letter "r", and invariably replace it by "l."

"Suppose other 'Melican man wake up, he make a low," continued Ah Sin, softly.

But the other 'Melican man did not wake up, and Bill Crane got away with his booty, as we already know. Cautiously the Chinaman followed him and ascertained where he intended to pass the night. It was at a moderate distance from the cabin which the two Chinamen had selected for their mining camp.

Bill Crane jumped from his horse, stretched his limbs, and gaped.

31

"I'm powerful sleepy," he soliloquized. "I can't go any farther tonight. I don't like to rest so near Miles, but I can be on the road before he wakes up. I guess it will be safe enough."

Crane, having made up his mind to rest, rolled himself up in his blanket, and stretched himself out, first tying his horse to a sapling. The place was retired, and he felt moderately confident that, even if he overslept himself, he would not be discovered.

"I'd like to see Miles when he discovers his loss," he said to himself, smiling at the thought. "He'll be ready to tear his hair and won't have the least idea how the gold dust was spirited away. You excel me in brute strength, John Miles, but one thing I am pretty sure of, you haven't got my brains," and he complacently tapped his forehead.

"There must be at least two hundred dollars' worth in that bag," he reflected. "It isn't a great haul, but it will do. It will last me some time and perhaps start me in something in Frisco. Bill Crane, you've done a good stroke of business today. You are entitled to a good night's rest, and you shall have it."

First, however, he concealed the bag. He did not think it safe to place it under his head as Miles had done. He scooped a hole in the earth near by, deposited the bag, replaced the dirt, and spread a few leaves over the top.

"No one will think of searching there," thought Crane. "Even if Miles himself surprises me here, he won't suspect anything."

Bill Crane felt that he was unusually sharp and crafty, and he felt great contempt for the stupidity of the man whom he had overreached. The time was not far off when he had occasion to doubt whether he had not overrated his own artfulness.

A pair of almond eyes, lighted up with mild wonder, followed closely all the movements of William Crane. When the bag was concealed, and Crane lay down to sleep, the Chinaman nodded blandly, and remarked softly, "All light! Me go find Ah Jim."

Ah Sin had to walk but half a mile to find the partner of his toils. Ah Sin and Ah Jim, though not related to each other, were as like as two peas. The same smooth face, the same air of childlike confidence, the same almond eyes, a pigtail of the same length, a blouse and loose pants of the same coarse cloth, were characteristic of both.

When the two met, they straightway plunged into a conversation in which Ah Sin had most to say.

Ah Jim listened attentively and was evidently well pleased with what his companion said. I am afraid my young friends are not well versed in the Chinese tongue and would not understand the conversation, however faithfully reported. They must infer what it was from what followed.

The two Chinamen bent their steps towards the resting place of Bill Crane. Ah Sin carried a bag of about the same size as the one Crane had stolen, which he carefully filled with sandy earth. With stealthy steps these two innocent heathen drew near the spot and looked searchingly at the recumbent form of the eminent representative of American civilization.

Ah Sin turned to Ah Jim with a pleased smile.

"All light!" he said. "'Melican man asleep."

A similar smile lighted up the face of Ah Jim. "'Melican man sleep sound," he said. "No wake up."

Quite unaware of the honor done him by the special Chinese embassy which had taken this early opportunity to call upon him, Bill Crane slept on. There was a smile upon his upturned face as if he were dreaming of something pleasant. He should have been a prey to remorse, if his conscience had done its duty, but Bill's conscience had grown callous, and gave him very little trouble. It was only when he was caught that he became sensible of a kind of mental discomfort which came as near to remorse as he was capable of feeling.

Reassured by the deep, regular breathing of the sleeper, Ah Sin and his friend proceeded to their work. The former drew a slender stiletto-like knife from a fan which protruded above the collar of his blouse, and, stooping down, began skilfully to remove the dirt which covered the bag of gold dust. From time to time he stole a glance at the sleeper to mark the first indications of returning consciousness. It was well for Crane that his sleep continued. A Chinaman does not set a high value upon human life, and the long stiletto would have been plunged into the 'Melican man before he was well aware of what was going on. Bill Crane's good genius saved him from this sudden exit by continuing the profound slumber in which he was repairing the ravages of fatigue.

The Chinamen therefore met with no interruption in their work. They drew out from its place of concealment the buried bag, and emptying the contents of their own poured into it the combined treasures of Miles and poor Tom. Then they filled the first bag with the worthless dust which they had brought with them and carefully reburied it in the ground.

They did their work so carefully and well that no one was likely to suspect that the bag had been tampered with.

Having done their work, Ah Sin and his friend smiled upon each other in bland satisfaction, which was further expressed by a low guttural chuckle.

"All light," said Ah Sin, with a nod.

"All light," chimed in Ah Jim, nodding in return.

A consciousness of lofty virtue could not have produced a happier expression upon any face than appeared on the mild countenance of the Chinamen.

"'Melican man much supplised when he wake up," remarked Ah Jim.

"Chinamen make much money," returned his friend.

The two enterprising visitors returned to their quarters, and concealed their booty in a safe place. Then they too lay down and slept the sleep of confiding innocence.

Bret Harte has not told us whether the heathen Chinee has a conscience, but if he has, neither Ah Sin nor Ah Jim experienced any inconvenience from its possession. Neither they nor Bill perhaps can fairly be taken as fair representatives of the different religious systems under which they were trained. Bill Crane could hardly claim any superiority over the heathen Chinee in point of honesty.

Bret Harte was an American author and poet who captured pioneering life in California.

CHAPTER VIII

BILL CRANE'S DISAGREEABLE DISCOVERY

It was five o'clock in the morning when Bill Crane opened his eyes. He felt refreshed by his night's sleep, yet under ordinary circumstances would have deferred getting up for at least an hour. But the consciousness that he had a treasure to guard, and the knowledge that he was at any moment liable to be called to account by the real owner, whose camp was scarcely more than a mile away, aroused him to exertion.

"I must get away while John Miles is still asleep," he thought to himself. "Let me get to Frisco first, and I can at once dispose of it, and he will never find me out."

Crane did not wait to prepare breakfast. That he could take on the road an hour or two later, when he felt safe from interruption. He rose and shook himself. This was his scanty washing. Next he must take the bag from its place of concealment, and then he could commence his journey.

While uncovering the bag, Crane did not discover that it had been tampered with, partly because it was still there. It was natural to suppose that, if discovered by a third party, it would be carried away. He did not even open the bag, not thinking it necessary.

"John Miles hasn't waked up yet," he said to himself with a smile. "When he does, there'll be some swearing, I'll be bound. You're a good boy, John Miles, but you ain't so smart as you think you are. I think I have got the best of you this time."

Bill Crane rode off smiling.

His course led him by the camp of the Chinamen. Early as it was they were astir. Ah Sin saw the rider, and he at once recognized him as the man he had robbed. How could Crane know that those pleasant-faced barbarians had served him such a trick?

"Hallo, Chinamen!" he said aloud. "Have they got out here already? I'll speak to them. Hallo, John!" he said, halting his horse, for even then every Chinaman was called John.

"How do, John?" replied Ah Sin, smiling blandly.

"My name isn't John, but no matter. What are you two doing?"

"Looking for gold," was the reply.

"Do you find any?"

"Velly little. Bad place."

"Have you been in San Francisco?"

"Yes, John."

"Why didn't you stay there?"

"Too many Chinamen--too little washee--washee."

"What have you got in the way of provisions? Mine are stale. I'd like to buy some from you."

"We have got a little lice, John."

"Got a little what? Oh, I know, you mean rice. Why don't you pronounce your English better?"

"Because Chinamen not 'Melican men."

"Then I suppose I may as well be moving on, as I can't get anything out of you. Oh, have you got any tea, John?"

"Yes, John."

"Got any made?"

Ah Sin produced a cup, for he and his friend had just prepared their breakfast, and being warm, Bill Crane gulped it down with a relish.

"After all, a man needs some warm drink in the morning," he said to himself. "How much to pay, John?"

"Nothing, John. 'Melican man welcome."

"John, you're a gentleman, or rather both of you are gentlemen, even if you are heathens. I'll remember you in my prayers."

The eminent Christian, Bill Crane, rode off from the Chinese camp, calmly confident of his moral superiority to the two benighted heathen whom he left behind him. Whether he remembered his promise to intercede for them in prayer is a little doubtful, or would have been, if he had had occasion to pray himself. It is to be feared that prayer and William Crane had long been strangers.

As Crane rode away, the two Chinamen exchanged glances. A gentle smile lighted up their yellow faces, and they were doubtless thinking of something pleasant. They exchanged a few guttural remarks which I should like to be able to translate, for they doubtless referred to Bill Crane, whom they had kindly supplied with a cup of tea gratis. Yet, perhaps, considering all things, it was the dearest cup of tea Crane had ever drank, since it was the only return he got for a bag of gold dust worth over two hundred dollars. But there is an old saying, "Where ignorance is bliss, 'tis folly to be wise." Crane was just as happy as if the bag really contained gold dust. But this happy ignorance was not to last long.

After riding five or six miles our traveller thought he might venture to dismount for rest and refreshment. He selected as his breakfast table the green sward beside a sparkling mountain streamlet. He dismounted, permitting his horse to graze while he took out the stale provisions which must constitute his morning meal. They were not very palatable, and Crane sighed for the breakfasts of old, the memory of which at this moment was very tantalizing. But he comforted himself with the thought that he had the means of making up for his enforced self-denial when he reached San Francisco.

This naturally led him to open the bag, and feast his eyes over his easily obtained wealth. He untied the string and with a smile of pleased anticipation peered at the contents.

His face changed suddenly.

Was he dreaming? In place of the shining dust, his eyes rested on--sand.

He hastily thrust in his finger, and stirred the grains. But nothing else was to be discovered. The bag contained nothing but worthless sand.

Crane stared at the deceptive bag in the most lugubrious astonishment. Surely the bag contained gold dust when he concealed it. There could be no doubt on that point, for he had opened it and seen the contents for himself. But in that case, how could such a change have been effected in one night? It had not been touched; so, at any rate, he believed. He had found it in the morning in the exact spot where he had placed it overnight, and yet--

Bill Crane took another look at the contents of the bag, hoping that he had been deceived by some ocular delusion, but the second examination brought him no comfort. He sank back, feeling in a state of mental and bodily collapse.

Never was poor thief so utterly bewildered as Bill Crane. He could almost believe that some magical transformation had been practiced at his expense. Was it possible, he thought, that John Miles, discovering his loss, had visited him and played this trick upon him? He could not believe this. It was not in accordance with John's direct, straightforward nature. Instead of acting in this secret manner, he would have sternly charged Crane with the robbery and punished him on the spot. Leaving him out of the account, then, the mystery deepened. It never occurred to Crane to suspect the Chinamen who had so hospitably furnished him with a cup of tea. Even if they had come into his mind, he would have been puzzled to account for their knowledge of his having the bag in his possession.

Bill Crane was decidedly unhappy. His glowing anticipations of prosperity, based upon the capital contained in the bag, were rudely broken in upon, and the airy fabric of his hopes dashed to the ground. He felt that fortune had been unkind--that he was a deeply injured man. Had his claim to the stolen property been the best possible, he could not have felt the injustice of fate more keenly.

"It's always the way!" he exclaimed in deep dejection. "I always was unlucky. Just as I thought I was on my feet again, this cursed gold dust turns to sand. Here am I out in the wilderness without an ounce to my name. I don't know what to do. I'd give a good deal, if I had it, to find out what became of the gold dust."

As he spoke, Crane, in a fit of ill-temper, kicked the unlucky bag to a distance and, slowly and disconsolately mounting his horse, plodded on his way. All his cheerfulness was gone. It was some comfort, but still scant, to think that John Miles was as unlucky as himself. Both had become penniless tramps, and were alike the sport of Fortune. There was a difference in respect to their desert, however. John Miles may rightly claim the reader's sympathy, while Bill Crane must be considered to have met with a disaster which he richly deserved.

CHAPTER IX

CLEANED OUT

John Miles slept long and awoke feeling refreshed and cheerful. He had a healthy organization and never failed to eat and sleep well. Like Crane, he had no washing to do, but sprang to his feet already dressed.

His first thought was naturally of his treasure. His heart gave a quick bound when he failed to discover it in the place where he remembered to have put it. In dismay he instituted a search, which, of course, proved unavailing.

"Who could have taken it?" thought Miles, large drops of perspiration gathering upon his forehead.

All about him was loneliness. He could see no signs of life. Yet the bag could not have gone away by itself. There was certainly human agency in the matter.

Miles confessed to himself with sadness that he had been imprudent to leave the bag where it would naturally excite the cupidity of any passing adventurer. That it must have been taken by such a one seemed evident. In that case, the chance of recovering it seemed slender enough. Nevertheless, John Miles decided to make an effort, hopeless as it was, to discover the whereabouts of his lost property.

"If it had been mine, I wouldn't have cared so much," he said to himself, with a sigh, "but poor Tom's money is gone too. I will make it up to him if I live, but I am afraid his father will be inconvenienced by the delay."

Miles made preparations for his departure, and strode away, looking searchingly to the right and left in search of something that might throw light upon his loss. Presently he espied the two Chinamen. Could they have taken it? He would at any rate speak to them.

"Good morning, John," he said, when he came within hearing distance.

Ah Sin bobbed his head, and repeated "Good morning, John."

"Do you live here?"

"Yes, we washee-washee for gold."

"Does anyone else live near by?"

The two inclined their heads and answered in the negative.

"Have you seen anyone pass last night or this morning?"

"Yes," answered Ah Sin. "'Melican man stay all nightee--over there. Chinaman give him a cup of tea this morning."

"How long ago?" asked Miles, eagerly.

"Two hours," answered Ah Jim.

"In what direction did he go?"

The two Chinamen readily told him.

Miles decided to tell them of the loss of his bag of gold dust. Possibly they could throw some light upon his loss.

"Someone stole a small bag of gold from me last night," he said. "I suspect it was the man you describe. Did he appear to have any such article with him?"

"Yes," answered Ah Sin, who, with natural cunning, saw that this information would divert suspicion from them. "It was so large," indicating the size with his hands.

Of course his description was accurate, for he had very good reason to know the size of the bag.

"He must have been the thief," said Miles, eagerly. "In what direction did you say he went?"

Ah Sin pointed to the west.

"I will follow him. It is on my way. If I catch the villain, it will be the worse for him."

"He velly bad man," said Ah Sin, sympathetically.

"That's where you are right, my heathen friend. Well, good morning, John. I am much obliged to you for your information."

"Velly welcome, John."

As John Miles rode away, Ah Sin turned to his friend Ah Jim, and remarked, "S'pose he catch him, he kill him."

"All lightee!" returned Ah Jim. "He velly bad man, he thief."

The two Chinamen exchanged glances. If they had been white men, there would have been a smile or a wink, but these children of Confucius looked so serenely virtuous, so innocent of guile, that the most experienced detective would have seen nothing in their faces indicating any guilty knowledge of the lost treasure. But, guileless as they seemed, they had proved more than a match for Bill Crane and his victim.

*****

41

John Miles rode away with a faint hope that he might overtake the man, whoever he might be, who had stolen his precious bag. In due time he reached the spot where Crane had examined the bag, and on discovering its worthless contents, had thrown it away. The thief had not taken the trouble to empty it.

When Miles saw it he hurried to it, hoping he might find some of the treasure inside. Of course he was disappointed and at the same time bewildered.

"This is certainly my bag," he said to himself. "Here are my initials, J. M. Then there are other marks well known to me. I could swear to it anywhere. But how does it happen that it is full of sand, and why has the thief thrown it away? That beats me!"

Miles decided that for some unknown reason the thief had transferred its contents to some other bag--perhaps his own--and then had discarded the original one, in wanton humor filling it instead with sand.

"He may have been afraid it would be found on him," thought Miles. "The marks on the bag would have been evidence enough to condemn him. By throwing away my bag he thinks himself safe."

His solution of the puzzle was ingenious, but as we know he erred in two respects. Bill Crane had not filled the bag with sand and thrown it away from prudential considerations, nor had he profited by the theft he had committed. He had been as badly outwitted as his victim, and the profit had gone to the bland and obliging Chinamen, who had thus far escaped suspicion.

John Miles slackened his rein and thought seriously and sadly of the position to which he was reduced. What was he to do? He was, in the expressive language of the country, "cleaned out," and brought to a pass where he must begin life over again, with the disadvantage of being seventy-five dollars in debt, for he was resolved that Tom's loss should be paid back to the uttermost penny.

Presently philosophy came to his aid.

"It might have been worse," he reflected. "Two hundred dollars is too large a sum to lose, but it won't take long to make up if I have any sort of luck. I wish I were in San Francisco. It may trouble me to get there without means."

When misfortune comes it is always best to look it manfully in the face and not to shrink from or over estimate it. John Miles had a strong, healthy nature, with a good deal of confidence in his own resources, and in an hour or two he was again looking hopefully forward to the future. Not that he cherished a hope of recovering his lost money. There seemed to be no way of identifying it, even if he should track the thief. One ounce of gold dust looks like another, and there is no way of distinguishing individual property in that form.

John Miles pushed on slowly. About noon he found himself threading a narrow canyon, shaded by gigantic redwood trees, with steep, almost perpendicular sides, with here and there a narrow streamlet descending in a cascade, and lighting up the darkened scene with its silvery reflections.

"This is a pretty spot, but it would be lonely to live here," thought Miles. "Yet," shading his eyes, "there seems to be a cabin of some sort. Is it possible that anybody lives in this canyon?"

Ten minutes' ride brought him to a rude cabin, with a gigantic tree spreading at a great height protecting branches over it. That it was inhabited was clear, for in front of it stood a strongly built, robust woman, who seemed to be nearing forty.

She bent a searching look upon the intruder, who bent his head courteously.

"Good morning, ma'am," said Miles.

"Good morning, stranger," was the reply. "Where might you be going?"

"I am on my way to the city. Am I on the right track?"

"I reckon so."

"Do you live here--alone?" asked John Miles, in some curiosity.

"It looks like it, doesn't it?" returned the woman. "I've been alone since my man pegged out."

"Is that long?"

"A matter of three weeks."

"I sympathize with you," said Miles. "You must be very lonely."

"Yes," said the widow. "Jim was good company, and I feel kind of lonesome without him, you better believe."

"There isn't much sentiment there," thought Miles. "She doesn't appear to be heart-broken. Do you mean to stay here alone?" he inquired. "Are you not afraid?"

"What's there to be afraid of?"

"Some tramp or adventurer might attack and injure, or at least rob you."

"Look here, stranger! Do you see that?" and the woman produced a revolver. "Do you see that shooting iron?"

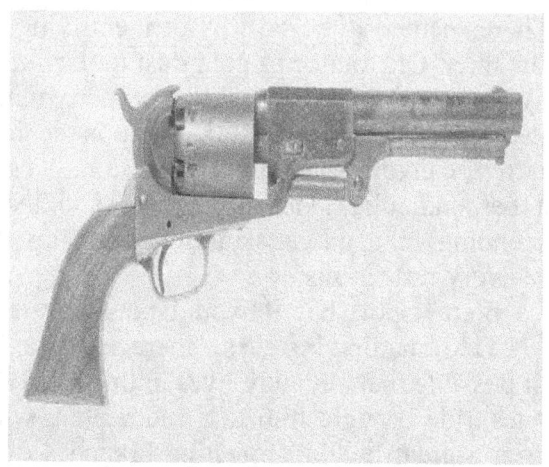

A revolver from the 1850s.

"It looks as if it might be a good one," said Miles, who began to think the woman better able to take care of herself than he had at first supposed.

"You bet it is! I know how to use it, too. If one of them tramps gets in front of it, and sasses me, he'd better say his prayers mighty quick, for he'll need 'em. He needn't reckon much on my being a woman. I can shoot jest as true as my man could when he was alive."

CHAPTER X

A CALIFORNIA WIDOW

John Miles eyed the woman curiously. There did not seem much that was feminine left in her. Life in the wilderness had made her as bold and self-reliant as a man. She was not compelled to plead for women's rights. She resolutely took a man's rights, and was prepared to maintain them against all comers.

"I rather think you can take care of yourself, ma'am," he said.

"You can bet your bottom dollar on that, stranger," said the woman, cheerfully. "Brown--that's my husband--knew what I was. We was ekal partners--Brown and me--and he knew too much to tread on me."

"I'm glad I wasn't Brown," thought John Miles. "When I marry, it'll be a woman, and not a man in petticoats."

"If you're hungry, stranger," said the woman, "just jump off that horse of yours, and come in. I can give you a square meal, and I reckon you haven't had one lately."

"You are right, Mrs. Brown," said Miles, dismounting with alacrity. "My provisions are dry and stale, and I shall enjoy a square meal amazingly. But I ought to tell you that last night I was robbed of a bag of gold dust, and I have nothing to pay you."

"Who asks for pay?" returned the woman. "I don't keep a hotel, but I'm tired of eating alone. I want to see how it seems to have a man setting opposite me agin. So come in, and I won't keep you waiting long."

"Thank you, Mrs. Brown. If you don't mind, I'll light my pipe, and sit out here till I've had a smoke."

"You can smoke inside if you want to. I always let Brown. It makes me feel better, now that he's pegged out, that I didn't deny him any of his little comforts."

"Clearly Mrs. Brown was a considerate wife," thought Miles, "but she doesn't look like a woman to fall in love with."

Tying his horse, he threw himself down on the grass and enjoyed the luxury of a smoke while Mrs. Brown was heard bustling about inside, preparing the square meal which she had promised to her unexpected guest.

Presently she reappeared.

"The victuals is ready, if you are, stranger," she said.

"I am ready, Mrs. Brown," said Miles, rising at once, and entering the cabin.

The cabin was rough and ill-adapted to a fastidious tenant, but it looked comfortable. What attracted Miles most, however, was a table set in the middle of the floor, covered with a substantial and appetizing meal. Mrs. Brown was a fair cook--perhaps her only feminine accomplishment. She placed Miles at the head of the table and seated herself opposite him. She watched his attacks upon the fare she had provided with evident satisfaction.

"I hope you like it," she said.

"Mrs. Brown, I haven't tasted anything so good for a long time."

She nodded, with a pleased look.

"Brown allus liked my cookin'," she said. "He had a good appetite most generally, and it was a pleasure to see him eat. It's kinder lonesome cookin' for yourself. Then, too, it takes away my appetite sittin' down alone to eat."

"You must be very lonely, Mrs. Brown."

"Yes, its lonesome like bein' a widder. I'm kinder used to seein' a man about the house."

"So I suppose."

"Be you a married man?" asked the lady, pointedly.

"No, ma'am."

"How old be you?"

"Twenty-eight," answered Miles, rather amused.

"Then you're old enough to get married?"

"Oh yes, I am old enough."

"Be you in love with any girl?"

"The old woman's getting curious," thought Miles. "However, I don't mind gratifying her curiosity."

"No, I'm not in love," he replied.

Mrs. Brown eyed him thoughtfully. She seemed to be revolving some plan in her mind.

"Take a good look at me, stranger," she said, bracing herself up, as if on exhibition.

"Certainly," said John Miles, considerably astonished.

"I want to ask you a few questions."

"Go ahead, Mrs. Brown."

"Am I hump-backed?"

"Certainly not. Who said you were?"

"Just attend to my questions, if you please, stranger. Am I squint-eyed?"

"Mrs. Brown must be crazy," thought Miles. However, he answered in the negative.

"Am I as homely as a hedge-fence?" pursued the widow.

"Has anybody been calling you so? If so, tell me who it is."

"Never you mind, stranger. Am I old and wrinkled?"

"Certainly she's out of her mind," thought Miles. "I must humor her."

"I think you are a very good-looking woman," he said, soothingly.

"No, I'm not," said the strong-minded lady, "but at the same time I ain't a scarecrow."

"Certainly not."

"Don't talk too much, stranger. I expect you're surprised at my questions, but I'll come to the p'int at once. I'm tired of livin' here alone. I didn't think I'd miss Brown so much. He wasn't any great shakes of a man, but he was better than nothing. He was company for me, Brown was, in the long evenin's, and I miss him. I've made up my mind to take on somebody in his place, and I reckon I'd like to engage you, stranger. Will you marry me?"

Mrs. Brown did not blush when she asked this extraordinary question. She was entirely self-possessed, and she could not have been cooler if she had been transacting an ordinary piece of business.

John Miles had never before received a proposal of marriage. He felt as awkward and confused as a young girl, and he began to hesitate and stammer.

"Really, Mrs. Brown," he began, "you have taken me by surprise."

"I expect I have," said the widow, "but I'll give you time to think it over. Brown left me I pretty comfortable, though I did more to get the property together than he. You wouldn't think it, perhaps, but I've got five thousand dollars in gold hid away somewheres near, and there's a claim not far away, that belongs to me, and will pay for workin'."

"I am glad you are so well off, Mrs. Brown," said Miles.

"If you marry me," continued the widow, "you can work that claim. You're a strong, able-bodied man, and a year from now, if you want to, we'll go to the city and settle down. I'm older than you, but a

---

47

matter of a few years don't make much difference. You were robbed, you told me?"

"Yes, of all that I had."

"How much was it?"

"About two hundred dollars."

"That ain't much."

"It's a good deal when it's all you have," answered Miles.

"If you marry me you won't miss it," said Mrs. Brown. "I won't give you my money right off, for you might run off with it, but at the end of the first year you shall have half of it. There's a parson a few miles up the canyon, at Dirt Hole, that will marry us any time we ride over. What do you say, stranger?"

It was an embarrassing moment for John Miles. He had no desire to succeed the deceased Brown, notwithstanding the little property he had left behind him. Mrs. Brown did not in the least resemble the wife of whom he had sometimes dreamed. But how could he decline without exciting the resentment of that singular female? He bore in mind that Mrs. Brown carried a revolver, and she might take a notion to shoot him down. He must temporize.

"Your proposal is a very kind and flattering one, Mrs. Brown, but I don't care to marry just at present. I want to go to the city and try my fortune. I've only lately arrived in California, and I am not ready to settle down yet."

To his relief Mrs. Brown accepted his objection in good part.

"No offence, stranger," she said. "I didn't know how you might feel about it. I've made you a fair offer."

"Indeed you have. The time may come when I shall return, and-
-"

"I won't promise to wait for you, stranger. Somebody else may happen along that'll take the offer."

"It would be too much to expect you to wait for me, I admit."

"All right, stranger. You've answered fair, and now we'll let the matter drop."

When Miles left the cabin he carried with him an addition to his stock of provisions, for which he was indebted to Mrs. Brown's generoristy. It was evident that she bore no malice, notwithstanding her suit had been rejected.

CHAPTER XI

BILL CRANE'S GOOD LUCK

About an hour after John Miles rode away from the widow's door Mr. William Crane came in sight of the cabin. He had strayed from the direct course and that had delayed him. Otherwise he would not have fallen behind Miles.

Bill Crane was in rather a melancholy mood. He had not got over his disappointment of the morning. He was exhausted and hungry, and he felt that luck was against him. When he saw the cabin, and the widow Brown sitting in the doorway, it instantly occurred to him that here was a chance to get a dinner. He had nothing to pay, to be sure, but he need say nothing about it till after the dinner was eaten.

As he rode up, he removed his hat, and said, "Good day, ma'am."

Mrs. Brown scrutinized the new-comer with critical eyes. She decided that he was not as good-looking as John Miles. Indeed Bill Crane never could have been accounted handsome, but on this point the widow was not exacting. She was looking for somebody to fill the place of her lamented Brown, and relieve her loneliness, and it was Crane's eligibility in this respect that she was considering. Beauty was but skin deep, as Mrs. Brown was practical enough to admit, and she was not overstocked with that attractive quality herself. Though Crane did not know it, the resolute, middle-aged female, from whom he hoped to obtain a gratuitous dinner, was making up her mind to offer him the position of husband.

"Good day, stranger," she answered composedly. "Are you travelin' fur?"

"I'm thinkin' of goin' to Frisco," he said, "but it's a long journey and I'm exhausted. If you have no objection, I'll stop at your place and see if I can rest a few minutes."

"You can stop if you want to," she said. "I don't see much company, and I like to see a new face now and then."

"So do I," said Crane, thinking a little flattery might help him, "especially when it's the face of a good-looking woman."

49

"I ain't good-lookin' enough to hurt me," returned Mrs. Brown, with a frankness which rather disconcerted and puzzled Crane, "but I don't mind you callin' me so. If you are anyways hungry, I haven't cleared away the dinner, and--"

"You are very kind," broke in Crane, eagerly. "I don't mind saying I am a little bit hungry."

"All right, stranger. If you'll wait long enough for me to make some hot tea and warm the victuals, you shall have a chance to judge of my cookin'."

Bill Crane was quite elated. He decided that the widow would not ask him for payment, thus saving him from embarrassing excuses. In due time he was called in and seated in the chair not long since occupied by John Miles.

"You're the second man that's dined with me today," said the widow.

"And who was the first lucky man?" inquired Crane, suspecting at once that it might have been Miles.

"I don't know his name, but he was a good-looking young man, who said he had had a bag of gold dust stolen from him."

"That's Miles," thought Crane, and he at once decided not to betray any knowledge of him.

"He was in bad luck," said Bill. "Did he know who stole it?"

"He didn't tell me. I don't think he knew."

"That's well," thought Crane.

"Did he say where he was going?"

"To the city."

"Do you live here all the year round, Mrs.----?"

"My name's Brown, stranger."

"All I can say is that Brown is a lucky man. Another cup of tea if you please, Mrs. Brown."

"You might not like to exchange places with him, for all his luck, stranger," remarked the widow.

"Indeed I would," said Bill, with a languishing look.

"He's six feet under ground!" explained Mrs. Brown, dryly.

"Dead?" cried Crane.

"Yes, he's been dead these three weeks."

"And you are a widow?"

"That's so, stranger."

"But you don't mean to stay a widow?" interrogated Crane.

"Well, it is kinder lonesome. It seems natural like to have a man round."

"I wonder if she's got any money," thought Crane. "I'll find out if I can."

"Yes, Mrs. Brown, I feel for you," he said. "A woman can't struggle with the world as a man can."

"I don't know about that, stranger. I can take care of myself, if that's what you mean."

"But a woman needs a man to protect and work for her," insinuated Crane.

"I don't need any one to protect me," said the widow, "and, as for support, I've got a matter of five thousand dollars laid by and a good claim that'll pay for the workin'. I don't think I shall need to go to the poor-house yet awhile."

Bill Crane's eyes sparkled. The widow Brown seemed wonderfully attractive in his eyes. He was willing to barter his young affections for five thousand dollars and a claim, even if the widow had been thrice as homely as she was. If he had known that Mrs. Brown was bent on marriage his way would have been clearer. His mind was made up. He would woo and win his fair hostess if he could.

"When did Brown die?" he inquired.

"Three weeks ago, stranger."

"You must miss him."

"Yes, he was a quiet man, Brown was. He never gave me any trouble, and it was natural to see him round."

"You must not mourn for him too much, Mrs. Brown."

"I shan't make a fool of myself," said the widow. "He's gone, and he won't come back. There's no use cryin'."

"She's rather a queer specimen," thought Crane. "She hasn't broken her heart, it seems."

"You ought to marry again," he said.

"I mean to," said Mrs. Brown.

"Well, that's frank," thought Crane. "There ain't any nonsense about her."

"Your second husband will be a lucky man, Mrs. Brown."

"Well, he'll have a good livin', and, if he treats me right, he'll get treated right too."

"This is a cold world, Mrs. Brown. I've been drifting about till I'm tired. I'd like to settle down with a good wife."

51

"If you want to take Brown's place, say so," remarked the widow, in a business-like tone.

Bill Crane was staggered by the promptness with which his hint was taken, but did not hesitate to follow it up.

"That's what I mean," he said.

"What's your name, stranger?"

"William Crane."

"You haven't got another wife anywhere, have you?"

"Of course not."

"I've got to take your word for it, I s'pose. I guess I'll take the risk. I'll marry you if you say so."

"How soon?" asked Crane, eagerly.

"Well, there's a parson a few miles from here. We can ride right over and be back by sundown, if that will suit you."

"A capital idea, Mrs. Brown. You won't be Brown long," he added, sportively. "How will you like to be called Mrs. Crane?"

"One name will do as well as another," said the widow, philosophically.

Crane wanted to make inquiries about the five thousand dollars and the claim, but he reflected that it might be inferred that his views were mercenary. It would be more politic to wait till after marriage. He did not understand the character of the woman he was going to marry. She understood very well that Crane was marrying her for her money, but she felt lonesome, and it suited her to have a husband, and she was willing to overlook such a trifle.

The widow had a horse of her own. Directly after dinner it was harnessed, and the two rode over to Dirt Hole, a small mining settlement, where the Rev. Pelatiah Pond, a Methodist minister, united them in the bonds of matrimony.

When Mr. and Mrs. Crane reached home, Bill ventured to inquire, "Have you got the money in the house, Mrs. Crane--the five thousand dollars, I mean?"

"It's put away in a safe place."

"You'd better let me take care of it for you, my dear."

"Not at present, Mr. Crane. A year from now I will let you have half of it, if you behave yourself."

"As your husband, madam, I insist."

"Stop right there, stranger--Mr. Crane, I mean," said the bride, decidedly. "Do you see that?" and she whipped out a revolver.

"Good gracious, Mrs. Crane! Do you want to murder me?"

"No, I didn't marry you for that, but I want you to understand that the money is in my hands, and I don't allow any man to insist. I may let you have some of it when I get ready. Do you understand?"

"I believe I do," murmured Crane. "I'm regularly taken in and done for," he reflected sadly.

But directly after their return Mrs. Crane prepared a nice supper, and Crane, as he ate it and smoked a pipe later, began to be reconciled to his new situation.

CHAPTER XII

TOM RECEIVES NEWS FROM HOME

Meanwhile Tom, happily unconscious that the money entrusted to John Miles had been lost, continued to work diligently at his claim. His success varied from day to day, but, on the whole, he was gaining. He spent nothing except for absolute necessities, and in spite of all temptations, he gave a wide berth to Missouri Jack's saloon. In this way he gained the ill-will of the saloon-keeper, who felt a certain portion of every miner's gains ought to find its way into his till.

One evening Tom met the saloon-keeper when out walking. The latter had not at that time given up securing Tom's patronage.

"Good evening, young feller," said Jack.

Tom answered the greeting politely.

"Why don't you come round to the saloon in the evenings? We always have a jolly crowd there. After a hard day's work it'll do you good to take a social glass."

"I would rather not drink, thank you," said Tom.

"You ain't afraid of a little drink, I hope, are you?"

"Yes, I would rather let it alone."

"Oh, you're too good to live," said Jack, in deep disgust.

"I hope not," answered Tom, smiling, "for I hope to live a good many years."

That was the last attempt Missouri Jack made to secure Tom as a patron. Our hero spoke in so decided a tone that he understood the uselessness of the attempt.

The interior of a saloon in California in the late 1800s

Two months passed, and Tom heard nothing from John Miles. He was not surprised or disquieted, for he knew that mails to the interior were very irregular, and, besides, Miles might not be fond of letter-writing. He took it for granted that the seventy-five dollars had been forwarded home and were now in his father's hands. He had saved as much more and would like to have sent that too, for its possession gave him anxiety, but there seemed to be no opportunity.

About this time he received two letters. The first was from John Miles, written from San Francisco. After acquainting Tom with his loss of the bag of gold dust, he proceeded:

"I should not have cared so much, Tom, had the loss been mine only, but it was hard to think that I had lost your money too and was unable to pay it back. I know, from what you said, that your father needed the money and that the delay would put him to a good deal of inconvenience. You shall have it all back, Tom, every cent, but you will have to wait awhile. On reaching Frisco I got work and soon saved up enough to pay the debt, when, as bad luck would have it, I fell sick, and before I got well all my money had been used up. Now I am well again, and at work, and if I have good luck I will be able soon to send on the money to your father. I know you will, understand the circumstances, excuse the delay.

"The very day I discovered my loss I had a chance to marry a fortune. You will stare at that and wonder how it happened. At a lonely cabin I made the acquaintance of a widow, who was looking out for a second husband. She was left with a comfortable property, which, with her hand, she was willing to bestow upon your friend, but she didn't tempt me much. I believe her fortune amounted to five thousand dollars and a claim. It would be a good chance for you, if you were old enough, Tom.

"I don't know when this letter will reach you, for the country mails--at least to such out-of-the-way places as River Bend--go quite irregularly. However, I hope you will get it after a while and won't be too much troubled about the money. If I live it shall be repaid."

Tom showed this letter to Ferguson.

"It's a pity, my lad, that the money was stolen," said the Scotchman, "but you'll get it again. John Miles is an honest man."

"I am sure of that, Mr. Ferguson. I don't know that I ought to make him pay it back, though. It isn't his fault that it was lost."

"That's true, my lad, and you might offer to share the loss with him, but I doubt if he would accept your offer. He will feel better to pay it all back."

"At any rate I will write him and make him the offer."

"That's fair, Tom, but you'll see what he'll say."

It may be stated here that Miles utterly declined to accept any abatement of the debt.

"I ought to have taken better care of the money," he said. "It's my fault, and I shall pay it in full."

The next letter was from home. Tom opened and read it eagerly. It was mainly from his father, but there was a note from each member of the family.

His father wrote:

My dear Tom,

We are glad to hear that you have reached California after a wearisome journey and are now at work. We have travelled so little that we can hardly realize that you are more than three thousand miles away from us, with so many mountains, plains and valleys between. Of course you cannot tell us much in your letters of your various experiences. I wish we could have you with us this evening and hear some of them from your own lips.

I am anxious to hear that you are succeeding in the object of your journey and that you will not find the stories of the rich gold fields greatly exaggerated. I do not myself believe all I hear, yet I think there must be gold enough to pay those who search for it diligently. You must remember, my dear boy, that hard work is better than luck, and more to be relied upon. Don't expect to make your fortune all at once by finding a big nugget, but work steadily, and you will meet with more or less success.

If you succeed moderately, I shall be glad you went away, for here prospects are not very good. Our little farm seems to be less productive every year. The soil is not very good, as you know, and I cannot afford fertilizers. This year the crops were not as good as usual, and we have felt the decrease sensibly. If there were not a mortgage on the farm, I could get along very well, but the interest now amounts to one hundred and thirty-two dollars annually, and it is hard to get that amount together. Next month sixty-six dollars come due, and I don't know how I am to find the money. Squire Hudson could afford to wait, but I am afraid he won't. The older and richer he gets, the more grasping he becomes, I sometimes think. However, I don't want to borrow trouble. If it is absolutely necessary I can sell off one of the cows to raise the money, and before the year comes round I think you will be able to help me.

Walter, though only twelve years old--his thirteenth birthday comes next month--helps me about the farm and is very useful in doing chores. He likes farm work and will be ready to succeed me in time. As for Sarah, she is a good, sensible girl, and she helps her mother in a good many ways. Though I am a poor man, and always expect to remain so, I feel that I am blessed in having good, industrious children, who promise to grow up and do me credit. I should not be willing to exchange one of my boys for Squire Hudson's son Sinclair. He is, to my mind, a very disagreeable boy, who makes himself ridiculous by the airs he puts on. I have seen him once or twice lately when he appeared to have been drinking, but I hope I am mistaken in this. He is an only son, and it would be a pity that he should go astray.

Tom looked thoughtful after reading this letter.

"Is it bad news, Tom, lad?" asked Ferguson.

"Times are hard at home, Mr. Ferguson," answered Tom. "Father is very much in need of money. It would have been a great help to him if he had received that seventy-five dollars."

57

"You have as much as that on hand now, Tom. If it isn't enough, I will lend you some."

"Thank you, Mr. Ferguson. You are a good friend, and I wouldn't mind accepting your offer, if I needed it. But father won't need any more than I can send him. Only I don't know how to get it to him."

"If you were in San Francisco, you would have no difficulty in sending the money."

"No."

"I've been thinking, Tom," said Ferguson, after a while, "that it might be a good plan for us to take a little vacation and visit the city. We have been working steadily here over three months, and the change would do us good. Besides, we might on the way come across some better place. This isn't as good now as when we began to work it."

"That is true," said Tom.

"Suppose, then, we stay a week longer, sell out our claim if we can, and start in the direction of the city."

"You and I?"

"Yes; we shall be better off without company."

"We had better not let Peabody know we are going, or he will want to accompany us."

"I could almost be willing to take him, poor creature, to get him away from that Missouri Jack, but, as you say, he would not be a help to us."

So it was decided that, in a few days, as soon as they were ready, Tom and Ferguson should leave River Bend.

CHAPTER XIII

A SPECULATIVE INVESTMENT

It leaked out after a while that Tom and Ferguson were intending to leave River Bend and considerable regret was expressed by the other members of the party. Tom was a general favorite. His youth and his obliging disposition made him liked by all except Missouri Jack and his set. It cannot be said that his Scotch friend was popular, but he was, at all events, highly respected as a man of high principle and rigid honesty. This was not the way the miners expressed it. They called him a "square" man, and that word expressed high moral praise. They all felt that Tom was going off in good company.

Before they went, the two had a chance for a speculation. Two weeks before, a man came to River Bend, across the country, with a horse and wagon, the latter an old express wagon, which he had brought round the Horn from some one of the Eastern States. What had induced him to take so much trouble to convey such bulky articles was not quite clear. Now that he was a miner he had no use for them, and at River Bend they were not saleable. This man, Abner Kent, came to Ferguson's tent, where he and Tom were resting after the labors of the day. He was a tall man, with a shambling gait and an angular face.

"Good evening," he said. "If you ain't busy I'll sit down a few minutes."

"We are glad to see you Mr. Kent," said Ferguson. "Tom and I were discussing our plans, but we've plenty of time for that. Come in. Here's a place for you."

"I hear that you are going to leave us, you two?"

"Yes, Tom has some business in San Francisco, and I want to see a little more of the country."

"How are you going?"

"We'll take the cars if we can find any," answered Tom. "If we can't we'll foot it."

"That's what I came to see you about. You know I've got a horse and wagon."

"Yes."

"Why don't you buy it? You'll go easier and quicker."

"We can't afford it," said Ferguson. "Poor men must walk."

"You don't see the point. When you get through with the team, you can easily sell them for more than you gave. It will be a good speculation."

"That will depend on how much we give," said the Scotchman, shrewdly.

"To be sure, Mr. Ferguson. Now about that, I'll be easy. They ain't any good to me here. I'll take--let me see--four hundred dollars cash. You'll maybe double your money inside of a month."

The team did seem cheap at this price, as prices of all articles in a new country are very much enhanced.

"Tom and I will talk it over and let you know tomorrow morning," said Ferguson.

"That's all right. It's a good chance for you."

When Kent was gone Tom asked, "What do you think of his offer, Mr. Ferguson?"

"I think it will be a good investment, Tom, and one that will make it less likely to be robbed than if we carried gold dust with us. You know how John Miles got robbed."

"I have only a hundred dollars," said Tom, doubtfully.

"I have enough to add to it, but I think we can get the team cheaper. I don't want to beat the man down, but a bargain is a bargain, and we must look out for our own interest."

"You know more about such things than I do, Mr. Ferguson; I will agree to anything you say."

"Very well, my lad, I shall be sure to consult your interest as well as my own. It will be very comfortable for us to have a team of our own."

"It will seem strange to me," said Tom, laughing. "What will they think at home when they hear that I have set up a carriage?"

"They might think it imprudent to invest all you had in that way, but we'll make money out of it yet, or I am sorely mistaken."

The next morning, while Tom and Ferguson were at work, Kent came up to them.

"What have you decided about the team?" he asked.

"We are not willing to pay four hundred dollars," said Ferguson.

"That's a fair price."

"It may be, but it will take all the money Tom and I can raise. You know it wouldn't be quite prudent for us to part with all our funds."

"I will take a note for part of the money," said Kent.

"That's very considerate of you, but scarcely prudent."

"Then don't you want it at all?" asked Kent, disappointed.

"Yes; we are prepared with an offer. We'll give you three hundred dollars."

Kent shook his head.

"That's too little," he said.

Ferguson remained silent. He wished to give Kent time to reflect upon his offer.

"Have you sold these claims of yours?" asked Kent, after a pause.

"No."

"Then add them to your offer, and I accept it."

This proposal struck Ferguson favorably. They could not carry away their claims, and very possibly no other purchaser might offer, as, except as regards to location, other places along the river-bank could be had without cost.

"What do you say, Tom?" asked Ferguson.

"I agree if you do, Mr. Ferguson."

"Then it's a bargain, Mr. Kent. I hope it'll prove satisfactory to both of us."

"I don't think you'll regret it. It's a good speculation."

A restored wooden wagon from a mid-1800s mining camp.

When the two friends had settled for their purchase, Tom paying one hundred and Ferguson two hundred dollars, our hero found himself left with twenty dollars, or its equivalent in gold dust, while his companion had about one hundred and fifty left over.

"We shall go off in style," said Tom, "riding in our own carriage. But there's one thing I have been thinking of. I want to send a hundred dollars home as soon as I get the chance. Suppose we can't sell the team?"

"Have no fears about that, Tom. I'll lend you the money if that is the case, but, mark my word, we shan't have it left on our hands, of that you may be sure."

The night before they were to start Lawrence Peabody dropped in. He was looking down in the mouth.

"How does the world use you, Mr. Peabody?" inquired Tom.

"Fortune is against me," said Peabody. "I'm tired of River Bend."

Tom glanced at his companion. He could guess what was coming.

"Won't you take me with you, Tom?" entreated the young Bostonian.

"You must ask Mr. Ferguson. He is the head of our party."

Peabody looked appealingly towards Ferguson, but the Scotchman shook his head.

"You mustn't be offended, Mr. Peabody," he said, "when I tell you that you are responsible for your own bad luck. You have had just as good a chance as Tom or I."

"Your claim was better."

"There was no difference that I can see, except that we worked, and you didn't. You don't expect gold to come to you?"

"You and Tom are more used to hard work than I," murmured Peabody.

"If you did not feel able to work, you should not have come to California. A man must work harder here than at home, and then he stands a chance of succeeding better."

"Then you won't take me?" asked Peabody, sadly.

"Are you in debt to Captain Fletcher for board?"

Peabody reluctantly admitted that he was but had no idea how much he owed.

"Fletcher tells me that he shall not trust you any longer."

Lawrence Peabody looked frightened.

"What shall I do?" he faltered. "I shall starve."

"You can't blame the captain; he knows that you spend the little money you do earn at the saloon. But he will give you a chance. There is no one to wash clothes in the camp, and we have all observed that you keep yours looking well. If you will set up a laundry, you can make more money than in any other way."

"But then I should be a common washer-woman," objected Peabody. "What would my friends in Boston say?"

"They won't hear of it. Besides, a man can do here what he would not do at home."

It may be stated here that Peabody, finding work absolutely needful, went into partnership with a Chinaman, who arrived at the camp a day or two later, and succeeded in making a fair living, which hitherto he had been unable to do. After he was employed, his visits to the saloon became less frequent. At times he was disturbed by the fear that his friends at home might learn the character of his employment. Apart from this he found his new business, with the income it yielded, not distasteful.

CHAPTER XIV

A NEW ACQUAINTANCE

Having made all necessary preparations, Ferguson and Tom set out on their way. They took a course differing somewhat from that chosen by John Miles, one object being to survey the country and find, if possible, a suitable place for continuing their search for gold. After their three months' steady work both of our travellers were prepared to enjoy the journey. Their road was difficult at times, from its steepness, and more than once they found it necessary, out of consideration for the horse, to get out and walk. But this only added to the romantic charm of the trip.

"It's like a constant picnic," said Tom. "I should like to travel this way for a year, if I did not feel the need of working."

"We might tire of it after a while," suggested Ferguson--"in the rainy season, for example."

"That would not be so pleasant, to be sure," Tom admitted. "Do you have such fine scenery in Scotland, Mr. Ferguson?"

"Our mountains are not so high, my lad, nor our trees so gigantic, but it's the associations that make them interesting. Every hill has a legend connected with it, and our great novelist, Walter Scott, has invested them with a charm that draws pilgrims from all parts of the world to see them. Now this is a new country--beautiful, I grant, but without a history. Look around you, and you will see nothing to remind you of man. It is nature on a grand scale, I admit, but the soul is wanting."

"I like mountains," said Tom, thoughtfully. "There is something grand about them."

"There are some famous mountains in your native state, New Hampshire, are there not, Tom?"

"Yes, but I have only seen them from a distance. They are not above thirty miles away from where I was born, but poor people don't travel in search of scenery, Mr. Ferguson."

"No, my lad, and there's another thing I have noticed. We don't care much for the curiosities that are near us. The people about here, if there are any settled inhabitants, care nothing about the mountains, I doubt."

"That is true. In our village at home there is an old man nearly eighty years old who has never visited the mountains, though he has lived near them all his life."

"I can well believe it, my lad. But what is that?"

The sound which elicited this exclamation was a loud "Hollo!" evidently proceeding from someone in their rear.

Both Tom and the Scotchman turned, and their eyes rested on a horseman evidently spurring forward to overtake them. Tom, who was driving, reined in the horse and brought him to a stop. The horseman was soon even with them.

He was evidently a Yankee. All Yankees do not carry about with them an unmistakable certificate of their origin, but Ebenezer Onthank was a typical New Englander. His face was long and thin, his expression shrewd and good-natured, his limbs were long and ungainly. In later life, with the addition of forty or fifty pounds of flesh, he would be much improved in appearance.

"Good morning, gentlemen," said he. "It seems kinder good to see a human face again. It ain't very populous round here, is it?"

"We haven't seen any large towns," said Tom, smiling.

"Where are you steerin'?" inquired the Yankee. "I'm expectin' to fetch up at San Francisco some time, if I don't get lost in the woods."

"That is our destination, my friend," returned Ferguson.

"Would you mind my joining your party?" asked Onthank. "It's lonesome travelin' by one's self without a soul to speak to."

"We shall be glad of your company," said the Scotchman, sincerely, for, though naturally cautious, he could not suspect the new-comer of anything which would make him an undesirable companion.

"Perhaps you'd like to know who I am," said the new acquaintance. "My name is Ebenezer Onthank, from Green Mountain Mills in Vermont. My father is deacon of the Baptist Church at home."

"I suppose you will take his place when you get older," said Tom, gravely.

"No, I guess not. I wonder what Susan Jones would say to my bein' a deacon!" and Ebenezer burst into a loud laugh.

"Is Miss Jones a particular friend of yours?" asked Tom, slyly.

"I should say she was. Why, I expect to marry her when I get home."

"I congratulate you."

"Don't be too fast. We ain't hitched yet. Say, boy, where do you come from?"

"From Vernon in New Hampshire."

"You don't say! Why, that ain't more'n fifty miles from Green Mountain Mills. Cu'rus we should meet so fur away from hum, ain't it? When did you start?"

"Seven or eight months ago."

"I've been in California six months. Does that gentleman come from your town?"

"My friend," answered the Scotchman, not without a touch of pride, "I am not an American. I am from the Highlands of Scotland."

"You be? Sho! Well, of course you can't help that."

"Help it, sir? I am proud of hailing from the land of Scott and Burns."

"Well, I guess it's a pretty nice sort of country," said Mr. Onthank, patronizingly. "I guess you'll like America best, though."

"I am by no means sure of that, my friend," said Ferguson, a little nettled. "America's all very well, but--"

"Why, you could put Scotland into its waist-coat pocket, and there'd be plenty of room left," said Ebenezer, energetically.

"I admit that, as regards to size, Scotland cannot compare with this country."

"Say, have you got mountains as high as them, or trees as high as that?" pointing to a gigantic redwood.

"No, but size is not everything."

"That's so. Vermont is a little State, but she's smart, I tell you. But you haven't told me your names yet."

"I am called Donald Ferguson, Mr. Onthank. My young friend here answers to the name of Thomas Nelson."

"Commonly called Tom," added our hero, smiling.

"Why, I've got a brother Tom," said Mr. Onthank. "Cu'rus, isn't it?"

Considering that Tom is by no means an uncommon name, it could hardly be called very remarkable, but Tom politely assented.

"Is he older than I am?" he inquired.

"Yes, my brother Tom is twenty-one years old. I expect he voted at the last town-meeting. I'm four years older than Tom."

"Have you been fortunate so far in California, Mr. Onthank?"

"Can't say I have. I guess I've wandered round too much. Been a sort of rollin' stone, and my granny used to say that a rollin' stone gathers no moss. I've got about enough money to get me to San Francisco, and I own this animal, but I haven't made a fortune yet. What luck have you two had?"

"Pretty fair, but it will take a good while to make our fortunes. We own this team, and that's about all we do own."

"A sort of an express wagon, isn't it?"

"Yes."

"Ain't goin' into the express business, be you?"

"Probably not. We bought it on speculation."

"That reminds me of old Sam Bailey in our town. He was always tradin' horses. Sometimes he made money, and then again he didn't. How much did you give?"

Tom told him.

"That was a pretty stiff price, wasn't it?"

"It would be considered so at home, but we hope to get a good deal more, when we come to sell it."

Their new friend kept on with them, amusing them with his homely sayings and original views of things. His conversation beguiled the tedium of the journey, so that all were surprised when the shadows deepened and suppertime came. Selecting a favorable place they encamped for the night.

CHAPTER XV

A GRIZZLY BEAR

Ebenezer Onthank was an early riser. He had been brought up on a farm, where, during a part of the year it was the custom for the "menfolks" to rise between four and five o'clock in the morning to begin the labors of the day. His old habit clung to him, and at five o'clock, when Tom and Ferguson were yet asleep, Mr. Onthank sprang from his leafy couch refreshed and vigorous.

Seeing his companions yet sleeping, he concluded to take a walk.

"It'll give me an appetite for breakfast," thought he, "and a chance to see something of the country."

As to the appetite, Ebenezer was generally well provided. Indeed, latterly his appetite had exceeded his means of gratifying it, and more than once he had longed to be back at his old home in the Vermont farmhouse, where the table was always generously, if not elegantly, furnished. If Ebenezer had a special weakness it was for doughnuts, which he called nut-cakes.

"If I only had a few of marm's nut-cakes," he had said the night before to his new-found friends, "I'd be a happy man."

"What are nut-cakes?" asked the Scotchman, puzzled.

"Don't you know what nut-cakes are?" inquired Ebenezer, astonished at Ferguson's ignorance.

"I never heard of them before," said Ferguson.

"Well, I declare! I thought everybody knew what nut-cakes are," cried the Yankee. "Don't you ever make 'em in Scotland?"

"Not that I ever heard."

"Then you don't know what is good. You know what they are, Tom?"

"Oh, yes," said Tom, smiling. "We often have them at home. Perhaps Mr. Ferguson would understand better if he heard them called doughnuts or crullers."

Thus defined Mr. Ferguson acknowledged that he had heard of them, and he thought he had once tasted one. Scotland, however, fell considerably in the estimation of Mr. Onthank, when he learned that his favorite article of food was almost unknown in that distant country.

"You Scotchmen don't know what is good," he said. "If you ever come to Green Mountain Mills, I'll get marm to fry a batch of nut-cakes, and you'll say they're goluptious."

This last word was not familiar to Ferguson, but the smack of the lips with which it was accompanied made it sufficiently intelligible. He assured Ebenezer politely that he hoped some day to accept his kind invitation.

When Ebenezer left the camp he had no definite plan of exploration. Everything was alike new to him, and it mattered little in what direction his steps led him. It was a charming morning. The sun had risen, and hill and valley were glorified by its slanting rays. The air was bracing, and Ebenezer, though neither a poet nor a sentimentalist, felt his spirits rise, as with vigorous steps he strode on, letting his eyes wander at will over the landscape.

"Looks kinder han'some," he said to himself. "I wish Susan Jones was with me now. Gals like to walk round and look at scenery and pick flowers and so on. As for me, a good field of corn suits me better than all the flowers in the world. They're only good to smell of; out here though I'd like a good 'claim' best. It seems cu'rus to think how much money you can get sometimes from a hole in the ground. Beats cornfields for profit, by a great sight, if you only get hold of the right place. I just wish I could find a big nugget, as big as my head. I guess it would make me the richest man in Green Mountain Mills. I'd be a bigger man than the old deacon. They'd be glad to make me selectman, and perhaps send me to Montpelier after a while to make laws. Well, there's no knowin' what may turn up. Why shouldn't I light on a nugget as well as the next man?"

In this pleasant channel the thoughts of our Yankee adventurer were running as he strode over the uneven ground, with all the vigor gained by his hardy training. But his walk was destined to be interrupted in a decidedly unpleasant manner. All at once he became conscious of a huge object, scarcely thirty yards away, whose attention he had already attracted. Mr. Onthank had been long enough in California to recognize in the huge, unwieldy figure--a grizzly bear!

Ebenezer Onthank was no coward, but it must be admitted that when he saw the eyes of the grizzly fixed upon him he turned pale, and his limbs trembled. He had heard from fellow-miners stories of the great strength and ferocity of this most formidable beast. The grizzly bear shows no fear of man. He is always ready to make an attack, even when not stimulated by hunger. Even the lion is crafty and cunning and likes to attack his enemy unawares, but the grizzly boldly advances to the attack without seeking to surprise his adversary. If out of humor it makes no account of odds, but will as readily attack a party as a single foe. Col. Albert S. Evans, the author of an interesting volume, containing sketches of life in California, says, "I am satisfied that an average grizzly could at any time whip the strongest African lion in a fair stand-up fight, while a full-grown bull is no more to him than a rat is to the largest house-cats."

Twenty-five years ago the grizzly was to be found in various parts of California. As the State has become settled his haunts have become contracted, but even now, as the writer just quoted assures us, he is still found in great numbers in the Coast Range Mountains from San Diego to Del Norte. In describing Samson, a famous specimen once on exhibition in San Francisco, we are told that "his strength was that of an elephant, and his claws, eight inches in length, curved like a rainbow and sharp as a knife, would enable him to tear open anything made of flesh and blood as you or I would open a banana."

The large and strong grizzly bear

Such was the new acquaintance who confronted Mr. Onthank and barred his progress.

"Jerusalem!" exclaimed the surprised and dismayed Yankee, and he instinctively felt for his rifle. But, alas! He had left it in the camp. It was thoughtless and imprudent to venture out unarmed, but the scene was so quiet and peaceful that no thought of danger had entered the mind of our unlucky friend.

The bear sat upon his haunches and stared at the intruder. Ebenezer, brought to a stand-still, returned his gaze. They were less than a hundred feet apart, and the situation was decidedly critical.

"I guess he wants to chaw me up for his breakfast," thought Ebenezer, despairingly, "and I don't see what I can do to prevent it."

The bear, however, seemed in no hurry to commence the attack. He surveyed our Yankee with dignified gravity, conscious that he had him at advantage. When Ebenezer felt for his rifle he uttered a low growl, being possibly aware of his purpose. Possibly he laughed in his sleeve (some of my young critics may suggest that bears have no sleeves) at his failure.

Ebenezer looked about him despairingly. No man will surrender at discretion to a grizzly, for he can hope for no mercy. But what could be done? Once subjected to the terrible hug, the life would be crushed out of him in less than a minute.

"If Ferguson and Tom were only here!" thought poor Ebenezer.

But the camp was at least two miles away, and his two companions, unconscious of his terrible peril, were calmly sleeping and not likely to awaken till he was a crushed and bleeding corpse.

In great crises the mind travels rapidly. I shall not attempt to record the thoughts that chased one another through the mind of the luckless adventurer. But they were by no means pleasant.

"I shall never see Green Mountain Mills again," he thought, with an inward groan. "I shall never marry Susan Jones or eat any of marm's nut-cakes. If I only had my rifle here, I'd make one effort for my life. I'd spoil the beauty of that ugly devil anyhow."

Still, as if charmed, he stood staring open-eyed at the grizzly.

Bruin, deciding that this had lasted long enough, began in a slow and dignified manner to approach the intruder upon his solitude.

This broke the charm. With a wild shout Ebenezer Onthank took to his heels and flew over the ground at a rate of speed which Weston, the champion runner, would scarcely be able to equal.

The grizzly accepted the challenge and increased his own speed, developing an activity hardly to be expected of his huge and unwieldy form.

It was man against beast, with the odds decidedly in the favor of the latter.

CHAPTER XVI

UP A TREE

The race between the Yankee and the bear was an exciting one, to the former at least. He was fleet of foot, and in a hundred yards' dash would have won without great difficulty, but in wind and endurance the grizzly excelled him. So, as the race continued, Mr. Onthank, looking back from time to time, was painfully conscious that his enemy was gaining upon him. The perspiration came out upon his face in large drops, and he panted painfully. He felt that the chances were against him, and he could almost feel in advance the fatal hug which would slowly press the life out of him. As he felt his strength failing he looked around him despairingly. Just before him was a moderate-sized tree. Though he knew that bears can climb, he gathered his remaining strength, seized a low hanging branch, and swung himself up just in time to avoid his persistent foe, who was close upon his heels. He did not tarry where he was but climbed higher up, until from a height of twenty feet he could look down upon the bear.

Bruin looked up placidly but did not begin to climb at once. Probably he was fatigued with his race. Moreover he knew that his intended victim could not get away. The latter was emphatically and literally "treed." The bear sat upon his haunches and complacently regarded the Yankee.

Ebenezer Onthank made himself as comfortable as he could under the circumstances. He was by no means easy in mind, however. He was "holding the fort," it is true, but the enemy was in force outside and evidently intended to remain. Worse still, he would probably after a while climb the tree, and this would bring matters to a crisis.

"You pesky critter! Why don't you go along about your business?" exclaimed the unhappy adventurer, shaking his fist at the foe.

Bruin deigned no reply, but continued to survey him with steady, unwinking eyes.

"If I only had a gun, I'd pepper you," continued Ebenezer. "I should like to put a bullet into that impudent eye of yours."

Though the bear had never received an English education, his instinct probably enabled him to understand the feelings of his intended victim, but he remained as placid as ever.

So an hour passed. At the end of that time the situation remained unchanged. The unfortunate Yankee was getting hungry, as well as tired of his somewhat constrained position. Bears probably have more patience than the human family, for Bruin had scarcely moved, except occasionally to wag his great head. He felt that in the game that was being played it was his adversary's turn to make the next move.

"I wish Tom and the Scotchman would find me out," thought Onthank. "What on earth makes them sleep so late?" he continued, irritably. "They must be naturally lazy."

He may be excused for feeling irritated, though there was no particular reason to expect his two friends to curtail their hours of slumber because he had done so. But he was not in a position where it is easy to be reasonable, and in his situation every minute seemed to him as long as five.

Meanwhile, in the camp, a mile away, Tom and Ferguson had awakened.

"How did you sleep, Tom?" asked the Scotchman.

"Tip-top. Did you rest well?"

"I have a gift of sleep," replied Ferguson. "But where is our Yankee friend?"

"I suppose he has taken an early walk," said Tom. "He will be back before long, I guess. We'd better not wait for breakfast for him. I'm hungry for one."

The two friends proceeded to break their fast, washing down the rather stale provisions with water from a spring near by.

"I wish it were coffee," said Tom. "I'm tired of cold water."

"Doubtless the coffee would be more gratifying to the palate, Tom, but it's likely the water is better for the health."

"I suppose you would refuse a cup of hot coffee, Mr. Ferguson, if it were offered you," said Tom, smiling.

"I don't say that, Tom. I would risk its effect upon my health for once. But, as we haven't got it, we may as well make the best of what we have."

Soon after their simple meal, which did not consume much time, Tom suggested to his companion that they set out in search of Mr. Onthank. He did not suspect that their missing companion was in trouble, but he thought that it would be pleasant to take a walk.

"You can go, if you like, Tom," said Ferguson, with characteristic caution. "I will remain behind to look after the camp."

"All right, Mr. Ferguson. I'll soon be back."

"Don't go too far away, my lad, and mind your bearings, so that you can find your way back."

"Never fear, Mr. Ferguson. It wouldn't be very easy to be lost here. I'll keep my eyes open and bring Mr. Onthank back with me if I see him anywhere."

Ferguson sat down and indulged himself in reading, probably for the hundredth time, Walter Scott's Marmion, of which he had a small pocket edition, while Tom went on his way.

A fortunate chance directed our hero by an almost straight course to the very tree where Ebenezer Onthank was still perched with the grizzly standing guard beneath. From time to time he looked about him anxiously, in the hope of seeing the approach of one of his travelling companions.

It was with a feeling of joy, not wholly unmingled with anxiety, that he descried Tom descending a hillock not many rods away. As yet it was evident that our hero had not caught sight of the bear and his prisoner. It was very necessary to put him on his guard.

"Tom!" shouted Mr. Onthank, at the top of his voice.

Tom heard the call in spite of the distance and looked about him, but he did not immediately catch sight of the speaker. It did not occur to him to look upwards.

"Tom!" shouted the Yankee again. "Here I am. Look up in the tree."

That time Tom's glance detected his companion, and, not yet having discovered the bear, he was led to wonder why Mr. Onthank had climbed the tree. As he was advancing incautiously, Onthank shouted again, "There's a cursed grizzly under the tree. Don't come too near."

Tom saw the bear, and he paused suddenly. He was startled in truth, for he had been long enough in California to be aware that it was a dangerous beast.

"Isn't Ferguson with you?" asked Onthank, anxiously, for he knew that a boy of sixteen, even if armed, was no match for the king of the California sierras.

"No, he's behind in the camp," shouted Tom, in reply.

By this time the bear became aware that there was a second intruder within his precincts. He turned his head deliberately and surveyed our hero. It is not within the range of the author to read the thoughts of a grizzly, but, from the indifference with which he turned away and resumed his watch, it may be inferred that he considered Tom too small game to merit his attention. This was rather satisfactory to our young hero, who was not ambitious to come in close quarters with so formidable an antagonist.

Startled as he was, Tom maintained his ground. He wanted to help Onthank, but he did not know how to do it.

"What can I do to help you, Mr. Onthank?" shouted Tom.

"Blamed if I know," answered the Yankee, helplessly. "I wish Ferguson were here. It won't do for you to attack the beast single-handed."

"Shall I go back for Ferguson?" asked Tom.

"I don't know. How far away is the camp?"

"It must be as much as a mile."

"While you are away the brute may take it into his head to climb the tree, and then I am gone up."

"Haven't you any weapon?"

"No."

"I'll fire at the bear if you say so."

"It would be of no use. If you missed, or only grazed him, he would make for you."

"I wish you had my rifle," said Tom.

"So do I. I'd let him have it straight in the eye. Have you had breakfast?"

"Yes."

"I'm as hungry as a bear--as this bear who probably wants me for his breakfast. Oh Tom, if I was only back at Green Mountain Mills once more, I'd be content to live and die there, and all the gold in California wouldn't bring me out here again."

Tom stood silent and perplexed. While he was considering whether he could do anything to help his friend, the bear slowly rose, approached the tree, and, grasping it between his paws, prepared to climb. He was evidently tired of waiting.

"He's coming, Tom!" shouted Onthank. "Oh Lord, what shall I do?"

CHAPTER XVII

AN EXCITING PURSUIT

Mr Onthank's reflections when the grizzly was slowly but steadily climbing the tree were by no means pleasant.

"If he once grips me, I am gone," he said, despairingly.

"Shall I shoot?" asked Tom, looking on in excitement.

"You might hit me," said Ebenezer, who knew nothing of Tom's skill as a marksman.

"No, I won't."

"I think I'll swing off," said the Yankee, "and join you."

Whether this was or was not a wise thing to do Tom did not feel qualified to decide. It was evident that Onthank must do something speedily, or he would be in the power of the bear. He waited nervously till Bruin was uncomfortably near, and then, seizing the branch with his hands, swung to the ground. The height was considerable, and the fall jarred him, but, quickly recovering himself, he ran towards Tom.

"Now we must run for our lives, Tom," he said, suiting the action to the word.

Tom fully understood the necessity, and followed suit, first hazarding a glance at the discomfited bear.

When the grizzly witnessed the escape of his victim he showed no excitement, nor did he accelerate his motions. He began deliberately to back down the tree. This required some little time, which Tom and his friend made the most of.

"Give me your rifle," said Onthank.

"I'd rather keep it," said Tom.

"I can make better use of it," said the Yankee.

"I don't know about that," said Tom. "At any rate I will keep it."

He felt that it was hardly reasonable to expect him, in the presence of such a danger, to give up his only instrument of defence.

"You are only a boy," said his companion, discontented.

"I can shoot," answered Tom, briefly.

Onthank was not in general an unreasonable man, but danger makes men selfish.

"Give it to me," he said, in a tone of authority, and he tried to wrest it from Tom's hands.

"You shall not have it," exclaimed Tom, indignantly. "Take away your hand, or I'll shoot you!"

Of course Tom was excited and would not have carried out his threat, but he was fully resolved to stand up for his rights.

Whether Ebenezer would have yielded the point, being stronger than Tom, is uncertain, but our hero shouted "Look out for the bear!" and the Yankee, in alarm, released his hold, and the two entered upon a race, in which the Yankee's superior length of limb enabled him to keep the first place.

Bruin was now on terra firma and was on his way, wagging his great head, developing an alarming rate of speed. Tom was somewhat hampered by the weapon which he carried, and he was getting out of breath. Onthank was three or four rods ahead of him. The situation had changed, and it was now Tom that was in the greater peril.

"Don't give out, Tom!" called out Ebenezer, encouragingly.

"I won't," gasped Tom, "if I can help it."

"Is he gaining on us?"

"Yes," returned our hero.

"Then I'll try another tree," said Onthank, and he caught a branch, and clambered up into a tree quite similar to the other in which he had been besieged.

Tom would gladly have followed his example, but the branch was too high for him to reach readily, and the grizzly was too near to give him adequate time. Poor boy! He began to despair and was at an utter loss what to do. To face round and fire at the foe seemed about all that was left him, but he wanted to reserve his fire to the last. He caught sight of another tree, of a larger trunk than the one which Onthank had ascended, and ran towards it, pursued by the grizzly. Then commenced a dodging game, which seemed to afford but a brief respite from destruction.

"This can't last long," thought poor Tom. "I suppose I must die."

In that brief time of peril many thoughts passed through his mind. To die at his age would be sad enough, but the thought that his expedition would be a failure, only involving his father deeper in difficulty and debt chiefly troubled him. The mortgage would be foreclosed, and his father and whole family deprived of their humble home. Onthank watched the boy's peril, unable to give him assistance. To do him justice he almost forgot his own danger in the more apparent and immediate peril of his young companion.

"Be careful!" he shouted, quite needlessly. "Don't let him grip you. Give it to him right in the eye."

Tom was so absorbed, and his mind so painfully occupied by his efforts to keep out of his enemy's clutches, that he was not conscious of the warning.

Active and alert as he was, the result was hardly a matter of doubt. He would tire sooner than the bear, and if he ran again he was sure to be overtaken. This, however, was what he did. Of course the grizzly instantly pursued him. Poor Tom breathed a prayer for help, though there seemed no chance of his prayer being answered, but sometimes God sends assistance when there seems no chance of escape.

The galloping of a horse was heard. There was a whirling sound, and Bruin, already within two yards of Tom, was jerked back, and brought to a standstill by a lasso which wound about his neck. A shout caused Tom suddenly to turn his head, and to his joy he saw a mounted Mexican vaquero, who had brought him timely relief.

Bruin growled angrily on finding himself balked of his prey. He was not disposed to yield to his new antagonist. Rising and sitting on his haunches he began coolly to draw in the lasso, against the combined strength of man and horse. The muscular force of a big grizzly is simply enormous. Usually he is attacked from two sides, two lassos being thrown around him. For a single antagonist he is sometimes more than a match, as seemed likely in the present case. The rieta was attached to the pommel of the saddle, and of course the bear, in pulling as he did, hand over hand, steadily brought the vaquero and his steed nearer. The horse, terrified, trembled in every limb, and tried to rear, but his strength was as nothing when opposed to the steady power of his massive antagonist.

elieved from the immediate attentions of the grizzly, Tom did not continue to run, but stood still, and, forgetting his own peril, remained an excited spectator of the struggle between the bear and the vaquero.

The Mexican, in an excited manner, shouted to him to shoot. This brought Tom to a sense of his duty. A third person had been brought into danger by an effort to give him assistance, and he was too manly to leave him to his fate. He raised his rifle, and, taking quick aim, fired. Our young hero was of course inexperienced, and it was only by a piece of good fortune that his bullet inflicted a serious wound, striking the bear in the throat. The blood began to flow and the grizzly, growling fiercely, slackened his hold on the lasso. The vaquero followed up Tom's shot by another, equally effective, and the powerful animal dropped to the ground, dangerous still if approached, but unfitted for pursuit.

The vaquero reined his horse back, and his dark face became illumined with a smile of satisfaction.

"He will do no more harm," he said in good English, but with a foreign accent. "The danger is over."

"Is the critter used up?" shouted Onthank, cautiously, from his elevated perch. "Is he defunct?"

"He soon will be," answered Tom. "I guess it will be safe to come down."

Ebenezer Onthank needed no second invitation. He "shinned" down the tree in a manner not unlike the grizzly and approached the spot where the huge foe was lying, the life-blood flowing from his throat.

"I'd like to kick you, you big brute!" said Mr. Onthank.

The bear slowly turned upon him his glazing eyes, and they expressed so much ferocity that almost involuntarily the Yankee drew back. The bear partly raised himself, and tried to drag himself towards his adversaries, but the effort was vain.

"He is one of the largest I have seen," said the vaquero. "See how strong he is!"

"It was lucky for me that you came up," said Tom. "He was almost upon me."

"I had about given you up, Tom," said Onthank, "and I thought my turn was coming next."

"We are much indebted to you, sir," said Tom, gratefully, to the Mexican. "You have saved my life."

The vaquero courteously expressed his satisfaction, and, remounting his horse, resumed his journey.

A vaquero in the early 1800s who has just lassoed an animal

"I never want to see another grizzly," said Onthank. "This one is enough for me, darn his ugly pictur'!"

"I quite agree with you, Mr. Onthank," said Tom.

CHAPTER XVIII

TOM'S OLD HOME

Leaving Tom for a time, we will cross the continent, and, a little earlier in point of time, look in upon Mark Nelson and his family at their humble home in New Hampshire.

For years Mr. Nelson had been struggling to provide a comfortable living for his wife and children. The struggle was not an easy one. His small farm was sterile, and yielded grudgingly its annual crops. Then the mortgage held by Squire Hudson imposed a burden of interest very hard to meet. Each half year sixty-six dollars must be raised somehow to satisfy the squire's demand. Though a rich man, with ready money in plenty, he never failed to call for his money on the very day it was due. Once or twice he had granted a delay of a day or two, but his manner was so unpleasant that the farmer, except from dire necessity, was hardly likely to ask a renewal of the favor.

The six months immediately following Tom's departure from home were not favorable to his father. There was a drought of considerable duration, which made the crops smaller than usual, and thus materially decreased the farmer's income. When the semi-annual interest became due, with the most energetic effort Mark Nelson had got together only thirty-six dollars towards it, leaving a deficit of thirty dollars.

"I feel anxious about tomorrow, Mary," he said, as the little family sat together the night before in the plain sitting room. "I have never been so much behind before with the interest."

"How much do you lack, Mark?" asked Mrs. Nelson.

"Thirty dollars."

"That is a good deal of money," said his wife, gravely.

"Yes, I don't know where to raise it. If Squire Hudson were only a little considerate. But he isn't, and, even if he were, I am afraid there is no prospect of my raising the money at present."

"You may get some money from Tom soon," suggested Sarah.

"I can't rely upon that. Tom will doubtless send when he is able, for he understands my circumstances and is a thoughtful boy, but it is going to take time for him to earn a surplus--enough to send on."

"He may find a big nugget," said Walter, the second boy, who eagerly read the letters from California which from time to time appeared in the weekly paper.

"He may, but the chances are against it."

"I was reading in last week's paper about a man finding a nugget worth over two thousand dollars."

"Such nuggets are as rare as large prizes in a lottery, I suspect," said Mark Nelson, who had a large share of plain common sense.

Walter looked rather disappointed, having made up his mind that Tom would certainly find a big lump of gold and come home rich.

"Don't you think Tom will find some gold?" he asked.

"Yes, I have no doubt he will gather some gold dust. I have no doubt, too, that he will earn more than he or I can do at home, but I haven't much faith in these extraordinary pieces of good luck."

"Still, Tom may find a nugget," persisted Walter.

"Yes, he may, and I shall be very glad if he does, but we must not build too many air-castles on that chance."

"I wish I could see the dear boy again," sighed his mother, looking up from the stocking she was laboriously darning.

"So do I," said Walter. "He would have a lot to tell us."

"California seems so far away," resumed Mrs. Nelson, "and he has no one there to look after him and mend his clothes--"

"And darn his stockings," said Walter, smiling.

"If he walked all the way across the continent," said Sarah, "I don't believe he would have larger holes in his stockings than you have, Walter."

"Oh, well, I exercise a good deal," said Walter. "Ask father if I don't."

"Walter will be more successful as a farmer than as a scholar," said Mr. Nelson. "He helps me a good deal."

"Tom was a good scholar," said Sarah, "and he was always ready to work, too. Walter will never astonish or electrify the world by his learning."

"I don't want to," said her brother. "It isn't in my line."

"That's true enough."

"Don't tease Walter," said Mrs. Nelson. "He helps your father a good deal, and he is not a dunce."

"Thank you, mother, for taking my part. Sarah is going to be a strong-minded woman. I should not wonder if she came out as a lecturer on 'Woman's Rights' some time. I think I see her, with a pair of iron-bowed spectacles on her nose, and her back hair tied up in a big knot, flinging her arms about, and--"

"That'll do, Walter," said Sarah. "It is an unusually powerful effort for you. I have no desire to lecture on 'Woman's Rights,' though I think they ought to have them all the same."

"I guess you'll get yours. You'll make your husband stand round, if you ever get one."

Sarah laughed good-naturedly and retorted, "I shall pity your wife, if she has to darn your stockings."

The next day about lunch time Squire Hudson walked up to the front door and knocked. His approach was witnessed, not without trepidation, for he was not an easy creditor.

The squire looked about him searchingly as he entered. He suspected that the interest was not ready, and the farmer's grave face confirmed his suspicions. That he was glad of this of course Mark Nelson did not dream, for he was not aware of his creditor's deep laid plans.

"A fine day!" said the squire, with suavity. "I hope you are well, Mrs. Nelson."

"Pretty well, thank you, sir."

"Have you heard from Tom lately?"

"Yes. He had just reached California."

"Then of course he could not say anything of his prospects?"

"It was too soon."

"You must miss him a good deal--all of you."

"I am thinking of him all the time," said Mrs. Nelson.

"To be sure, that is natural in a mother. But if the boy does well, that will repay you hereafter."

"If I only felt sure he would do well."

"Oh, he is young and industrious. He will be sure to make his way. He'll like it too. Why, my Sinclair envies him the chance of leaving home. He wanted to go with him."

"Sinclair would not like to go in the same way as Tom, with the prospect of having to work hard after he got there," said Mark Nelson.

"To be sure not, neighbor Nelson. My boy has never been brought up to work. My circumstances--ahem!--have not made it necessary."

"Sinclair is fortunate in having a rich father," said the farmer.

"So I tell him," said the squire, complacently. "His fortune is already made."

"What are you going to do with him, squire?"

"Oh, I shall make a professional man of him--a lawyer, most likely," said the rich man, complacently. "I can give him a suitable income till he gets into a paying practice."

"That will be a good many years," thought Sarah, "unless Sinclair works harder than he has lately at school," but the shrewd young lady kept this thought to herself.

One by one wife and children left the room, for it was well understood that the squire came on business and would be likely to desire a private interview with the farmer. They went into the kitchen, closing the door behind them, and awaited anxiously the result of the interview.

"I do hope Squire Hudson will be considerate," said Mrs. Nelson, anxiously.

"I am afraid he won't be, mother," said Sarah. "He is a hard man."

"Sinclair puts on no end of airs," said Walter. "By the way he struts round you would think he owned the whole town. You had better set your cap for him, Sarah, for he will be rich some day."

"I would rather be an old maid than marry him," said Sarah, decidedly.

"Very likely your wish will be gratified," said her brother.

Mrs. Nelson did not smile at this sally, for her mind was too full of anxiety.

CHAPTER XIX

A MODERN SHYLOCK

"I believe your interest falls due today, Mr. Nelson," said the squire, when he found himself alone with his debtor.

"Yes," answered the farmer, slowly. It was not very likely to slip his mind.

"I suppose you have the money ready," continued the squire, who supposed no such thing.

"I have a part of it ready," said Mark Nelson, with an effort.

"A part," repeated his creditor, with a frown.

"Yes. I can give you thirty-six dollars today."

"Only thirty-six dollars! The amount due is sixty-six."

"I know it, Squire Hudson, but this has been a bad year for the farmers, as you probably know. Owing to the drought, my crops fell off at least one quarter."

"I can't help that," said the squire, coldly.

"If you will be a little patient," said Mr. Nelson, uneasily.

"Neighbor Nelson," said his creditor, interrupting him, "I wish to ask you one question. When I lent you money on mortgage was there a stipulation that if there was a drought I was to wait for my just interest?"

"No, Squire Hudson."

"To be sure not. I would not of course lend you money on any such terms. It was understood that my interest was to be paid semi-annually--was it not so?"

"Yes, but--"

"Wait a moment. You must certainly agree that I am entitled to prompt payment. A bargain is a bargain."

"I don't dispute it, Squire Hudson, and I have tried to be ready for you, but in spite of all my efforts I am thirty dollars short."

"Do you expect me to be content with this explanation?"

"I think you are rather hard on me, squire. It isn't as if I had the money and objected to pay. I am a poor man, but no one ever lost a dollar by me, and I don't mean that any one shall while I have my life and strength."

"That's all very well, but it won't make up the thirty dollars in which you are delinquent."

"What would you have me do? I cannot make money."

"I wouldn't give much for an investment when the interest is delayed. It is no longer worth its face. If any of my railroad bonds defer their usual interest they at once drop in value."

"I know very little of railroad bonds, never having any money to invest in them, but I think my farm will be full security for all the money I owe you."

"Suppose I should foreclose--you would consider it an unkind thing and a great hardship, wouldn't you?"

"It would take away my means of supporting my family. I don't think you would go to extremes for the sake of thirty dollars."

"It isn't the amount of money, neighbor Nelson, that is to be considered. It is the principle that is involved."

This is a very common pretext with men who have made up their minds to do a mean thing. Generally speaking it is false, and the money is the first consideration.

"Will you give me two months to pay the balance of interest?" asked Mark Nelson.

"What better prospect have you of being able to pay me then?"

"As soon as Tom has any money to send, he will remit to me. I think it probable that I shall hear from him in the course of two months."

"If that is your reliance," said the squire, shrugging his shoulders, "I am afraid you are leaning upon a broken reed. I know boys pretty well, and I fancy Tom will find a use for all the money he earns."

"You don't know him, Squire Hudson. He is a very conscientious boy, and he understands very well the sacrifice I made in raising money to send him to California. He is not very likely to forget that."

"It seems to me that the sacrifice was mine," said the squire, with a half sneer. "If I remember rightly, I advanced the money which he took away with him."

Mark Nelson flushed, and he answered warmly, "You did advance the money, Squire Hudson, but I gave you security for it."

"And the very first interest that has come due you are not prepared to meet. You can't blame me for feeling a little doubt as to the wisdom of my advance."

"Are you very much in need of the thirty dollars?" asked Mr. Nelson, nettled at the squire's tone.

What do you mean, sir?"

"Is it subjecting you to any great inconvenience to wait a couple of months for it? That is what I mean."

"My circumstances are not such," returned the squire, haughtily, "as to make me feel even the loss of thirty dollars."

"I wish I could say the same, but I cannot. Since, then, it will occasion you no inconvenience, I ask you as a favor that you will let the balance rest for two months."

Squire Hudson saw that he was cornered, but none the less was he disposed to yield the point. He even felt provoked with the farmer for having forced from him an acknowledgment that he did not need the money he so persistently demanded.

"I told you before," he said, "that it was not the amount of money, but the principle, that I care for. You cannot have forgotten this."

"I don't see how any principle is involved, Squire Hudson."

"You look at the matter solely from a debtor's point of view. If you held the mortgage, instead of myself, you would change your view very quickly."

"I don't think I should," said the farmer, slowly. "I would be considerate to a poor neighbor, even if it did inconvenience me a little."

"The poor neighbor should not have borrowed money on which he was unable to pay interest," said Squire Hudson, severely.

"How could I anticipate the drought that has diminished my crops?" said Mark Nelson, with spirit.

"That is neither here nor there. You knew that the interest must be paid, drought or no drought, crop or no crop."

"I cannot argue with you further, since you refuse to consider circumstances over which I have had no control. You refuse to grant me any delay?"

"I do."

"Since I have not the money to pay you, will you tell me what you require?"

"How many cows do you keep?"

"Three."

"You can give me one of these, and I will consider it an equivalent for the thirty dollars."

"Do you require this?" asked the farmer, uneasily.

"Yes, unless you have some other satisfactory arrangement to propose."

"I am afraid I have nothing else which you would regard as satisfactory. The loss of a cow will diminish my income. Instead of three, I ought to have four or five. I shouldn't like to be reduced to two."

"Very likely not, but an honest man is willing to make a sacrifice in order to meet his just liabilities. Besides, you expect to have the money, you say, in a couple of months. When it has come, you may have your cow back, on paying two months' interest on the deferred payment. That is only fair."

"Say no more, Squire Hudson," said the farmer. "I must, of course, consent to this arrangement since you insist upon it. How soon do you wish for the cow?"

"You had better let your son Walter drive it over this afternoon."

"He is losing no time," thought Mark Nelson, bitterly. "He does not even appear to be willing that I should have the benefit of this night's milking."

"You may send me Whiteface," continued Squire Hudson, who knew that this was the most valuable of the three cows.

"That is my best cow," protested the farmer.

"That makes little difference, as you expect to redeem it in two months."

Mark Nelson was silent. He felt indignant with Squire Hudson for his cruel exaction, but he felt that he was in his power, and that he must submit to his exactions.

"You will attend to this matter?" asked the squire, as he rose and prepared to go.

"Yes," answered the farmer, coldly.

When his creditor was gone he went into the kitchen and acquainted the family with what had passed. Great were the grief and indignation of the children, and Walter expressed a desire that Squire Hudson might lose all his property as a fitting reward for his meanness.

"Heaven help me if I can't meet the next interest!" said Mark Nelson, later in the day, to his wife.

"Don't be too much troubled about the future, Mark," said his wife, who was of a more hopeful temperament than her husband. "I am sure that you will get some help from Tom before six months are over."

"I hope so," answered her husband, but for the rest of the day he was very grave.

Walter drove over Whiteface, at his father's request, but he came near crying, stout boy as he was, at the loss of the faithful animal which his father had reared from a calf.

CHAPTER XX

AT SACRAMENTO

After his escape from the grizzly Tom had no further adventures of an exciting character. One afternoon he and his companions arrived at Sacramento. It was but a small settlement, but it was more town-like than any place they had yet seen in California. They drove to a two-story frame building, which was the chief hotel in the town. Taking the precaution to inquire the price of board and lodging, they were dismayed by the extravagance of the charges. Tom saw that his reserve fund of twenty dollars would scarcely last him forty-eight hours.

A bird's eye view of Sacramento in 1857

"I can't stay here, Mr. Ferguson," he said. "I will take my chances and camp out, if necessary."

"I agree with you, lad. I'm not inclined to waste my substance on luxurious living."

"There won't be much luxurious living, I guess," said Ebenezer Onthank, who, with Yankee curiosity, had already visited the kitchen and obtained some idea of the fare to be expected. "I kin get better board at Green Mountain Mills for three dollars a week, and folks are darned glad to accommodate you for that price. These chaps seem to think and act as if we were made of money."

"I wish some of your Green Mountain Mills boarding-houses were here," said Tom. "I could save plenty of money then."

"Well, gentlemen, do you want to stay here?" inquired the landlord.

"We'd like to, squire, but not bein' millionaires I guess we'll have to put it off till times are better."

"Just as you say," said the landlord, indifferently. "There's others waiting for the only room I have empty." Then, noticing for the first time the express wagon which Tom had left outside, he asked, in a tone of interest, "Who owns that team?"

"It belongs to this boy and myself," answered Ferguson.

"Where did it come from?"

"The States."

"You don't want to sell, do you?"

Tom was about to reply in the affirmative, but the Scot, more shrewd, answered indifferently, "We may sell it when we get to San Francisco."

"I need just such a team as that," said the landlord, eagerly. "I'll give you a good price for it. You can go down the river to Frisco."

"I suppose we might," said Ferguson, slowly, "if it was worth our while."

"What'll you take, cash down?" inquired the landlord, earnestly.

"Nay, my friend, I prefer to hear your views as to the price."

"I will give you eight hundred dollars for the wagon."

This was certainly an excellent profit, for but three hundred had been paid for horse and wagon. Tom's heart beat fast with excitement, for he remembered that one-third of the money would come to him. If it had depended upon him he would have clinched the bargain at once, but he wisely left the matter in the hands of his companion and partner.

"That seems a fair offer," said Ferguson, "but I think we may as well wait till we reach San Francisco. Besides, we want to sell the horse, too."

"I will give you a thousand dollars for the two," said the landlord.

A man with his pantaloons tucked in his boots, a coarse woolen shirt, and a wide-brimmed sombrero, which overshadowed a face bearing a beard of a week's growth, was leaning against the door-post.

"Landlord," said he, "I see your price, and I'll go two hundred better."

Tom stared at the speaker in surprise. He looked like a man who would have found it hard to raise twelve dollars, yet he had made an offer of twelve hundred. Our hero did not learn till afterwards that the man had "struck it rich" at the mines, sold out his claim for ten thousand dollars, and for the time being was the lucky possessor of a large bank account.

"Now, Tom Scott," expostulated the landlord, "this ain't fair. I want the wagon more'n you do, and you're a-raisin' the price on me."

"How do you know that?" drawled Scott. "I've got a pile, and I mean to take it easy while it lasts. I'm going back to the mines like a gentleman, with my own team, you bet, if I've got money enough to buy one."

The landlord was satisfied that, if he wanted the team, he must outbid his competitor, and he advanced his offer to thirteen hundred dollars. But Tom Scott was not terrified. His money had come easily, and he would not let two or three hundred dollars stand in the way of his wishes.

"I'll go fifteen," he drawled.

The landlord shrugged his shoulders, and said, in a disappointed tone, "You'll have to take it, Scott. You've gone ahead of my pile."

"Well, stranger, is it a bargain?" asked Scott.

The Scotchman, though inwardly elated as well as astonished at the extraordinary offer he had received, answered quietly, "If my partner agrees."

"I guess we'd better sell," said Tom, trying not to betray his inward satisfaction.

"All right," said Scott, appearing to be well pleased. "You can have your money when you want it. If you are going to Frisco, I'll give you an order on my banker there."

"Tom Scott's a square man, and his order will fetch the money," said the landlord, observing Ferguson's prudent hesitation.

"That is satisfactory," replied Ferguson.

In five minutes more the business was concluded, and Ferguson and Tom, longing to congratulate each other on their good fortune, walked off together.

"We're in luck, Mr. Ferguson," said Tom. "I don't know whether I stand on my head or my heels. I never expected such a price."

"Twelve hundred dollars is a great profit," said Ferguson. "I almost doubt whether we are justified in asking such an extortionate price of the poor man."

"He is pleased with his bargain, and I don't think we need to trouble ourselves about that," answered Tom. "Besides, you know we can't compare prices with those at home."

"No doubt there is reason in what you say, my lad, but it's not easy at first to make allowance for the difference."

"That's so, Mr. Ferguson. When shall we go to San Francisco?"

"We will go tomorrow, if we can. I suppose you will wish to send some money to your father."

"Yes, I am in a hurry to send to him, for I am sure he needs it already. I can hardly realize that I am worth five hundred dollars."

"Five hundred?"

"Yes, I had a third share in the team."

"That isn't my way of looking at it, Tom."

"Is it possible Mr. Ferguson would cheat me out of my fair share?" thought Tom, but he only harbored the suspicion for an instant. He had seen too much of his friend to believe such a thing, and he quietly waited for an explanation.

"I'll tell you how I propose that we divide it, Tom. First we'll take out the money each of us put in, one hundred for you and two hundred for me, and then we'll divide the profit equally."

"But," protested Tom, "you are entitled to two-thirds."

"Then I won't take it," said Ferguson, decidedly. "I only want half of the profit. That will give me eight hundred dollars, and that ought to satisfy me."

"And I shall have seven hundred," said Tom, his eyes sparkling.

"Precisely."

"How kind you are, Mr. Ferguson!" exclaimed Tom, eagerly seizing the Scotchman's hand.

"No, my lad. I am only just. I am glad to help a boy who is working for his father and family."

"I shouldn't deserve to succeed if I didn't," said Tom, earnestly.

"Always bear that in mind, my lad, and God will smile on your efforts and raise you up friends."

In spite of the high price, Tom and his partner felt justified now in stopping over night at the hotel where they had met with such a piece of good luck, and the next day started down the river for San Francisco.

94

CHAPTER XXI

TOM BUYS A BUSINESS

It was an interesting moment for our two friends when they landed in San Francisco. The future Western metropolis was only a town of scattered wooden and adobe houses, with irregular streets and a general lack of uniformity in its buildings, but everybody seemed on the alert. The number of drones was wonderfully small; even the constitutionally lazy could not resist the golden incentives to labor. Money was looked upon with very different eyes there than in the East. No one took the trouble to dispute prices, and a man who landed with an article rare or desirable could often obtain twenty times its value. Within ten minutes of his arrival Tom witnessed a case of this kind.

Just as he was entering Montgomery street he noticed a man-- evidently a new-comer--with a fine bunch of pineapples in his hand. He had just arrived in the steamer Columbus, then anchored out in the stream.

"I shouldn't mind having one of those pineapples," said Tom to Ferguson.

"Doubtless they are high-priced, being a rarity," said the Scotchman.

Just then a passer-by, attracted like Tom, and feeling a similar longing, stepped up to the new-comer.

"Are those pineapples for sale?" he asked.

"Yes, if you'll pay enough," was the half-jocular reply.

"Name your price."

"Ten dollars."

"Here is your money," and he put a gold piece into the hand of the astounded passenger, which represented ten times the sum he had paid for the fruit at San Blas.

"That's a pretty steep price," said Tom, "for six pineapples."

"It is very wasteful to spend such a sight of money to pamper the appetite," said the canny Scot. "Truly, a fool and his money are soon parted."

He was destined to be still more surprised. The purchaser within five minutes transferred half his purchase to another for fifteen dollars.

"Gold seems to be plenty here," said Tom.

"I hope all provisions are not as high," said Ferguson, "or we shall soon have a chance to spend all we have."

"Where shall we go first?" asked Tom.

"We had better go to a public house and secure a lodging," said Ferguson.

"I wish I knew someone here to direct me."

Scarcely had Tom uttered these words than he cried out in surprise, "Why, there's John Miles!"

They were passing a little, unpainted, wooden building, of one and a half stories, used as a grocery. A German name was on the sign, but behind the rough counter stood the familiar form of John Miles.

Tom dashed into the store, followed by his more dignified companion.

"How are you, John?" he exclaimed.

"Why, if it isn't Tom," returned Miles, his face showing the joy he felt. "And here's Mr. Ferguson, too."

Then there ensued a hearty shaking of hands, followed by the question, "When did you get here?"

"About twenty minutes ago."

"And you came straight to me. That's good."

"So it is, but it's an accident. We had no idea where you were. So you are a grocer, John. Is the place yours?"

"If it is, then I've changed my name," said Miles, pointing to the sign bearing the name:

JOHN SCHINKELWITZ.

"The first name's right, at any rate," said Tom, laughing. "I suppose you are the clerk, then."

"Yes."

"How long have you been here?"

"Four weeks."

"Is it a good business?"

"Very good. My Dutch friend pays me five dollars a day, and I sleep here."

"Among the groceries?"

"Yes. It saves me the expense of a bed outside, and that is a good deal. I haven't saved quite enough to pay you yet, Tom, but I can soon."

"No hurry, John. I have been lucky since I saw you."

"I am glad to hear it, Tom. Did the claim prove more productive?"

"No, but I have been speculating. Guess how much money I have with me."

"A hundred and fifty dollars."

"More."

"Two hundred."

"More yet."

"Not three hundred, Tom?"

"I won't make you guess any more. I have seven hundred dollars. No wonder you look surprised. I'll tell you how I made it," and Tom repeated the story of his purchase and its profitable sale.

"I am not so much surprised now," said Miles, "for in this country a man will have what he takes a fancy to, no matter what it costs. I am glad the good luck came to you and Mr. Ferguson. I shouldn't mind having that amount of money myself."

"What would you do with it?"

"I would buy out my employer, and then I could make money fast."

"Does he want to sell?"

"Yes, he wants to go to the mines."

"Would he sell for such a small sum?"

"Yes. There isn't much of a stock, but we are constantly replenishing. I tell you what, Tom, you buy him out, and I'll manage the business."

"Are you in earnest, John?"

"Certainly I am."

"But I want to send some money home," objected Tom.

"How much?"

"A hundred dollars at least."

"I'll lend you the hundred, my lad," said Ferguson, "and fifty more, and you can take your own money and buy the business. I don't favor acting hastily, in general, but I have faith in our friend here, and I am led to believe that the enterprise will be a profitable one."

"You'll be my partner, Tom, and I'll give you a third of the profits without your doing a thing. If you work with me, you shall have as much more as will be satisfactory."

"I would rather go back to the mines, John, and leave you to manage this business by yourself. A quarter of the profits will satisfy me."

"No, it shall be a third. As you furnish the capital, that is only fair."

"We may be counting our chickens too soon. Perhaps your Dutch friend, whose name I can't pronounce, won't sell."

"Here he is to speak for himself."

A short German, with a ponderous frame, and a broad, good-humored face, here entered the grocery, panting with the exertion of walking, and looked inquiringly at Tom and the Scotchman.

"Herr Schinkelwitz, this is my friend, Tom Nelson," said Miles.

"Glad to see you, mine vriend," said the German, addressing Ferguson.

"No, that is Mr. Ferguson," said Miles, smiling. "I should have introduced him first."

"Wie gehts, Herr Ferguson?" said the grocer. "You have one strange name."

"Your name seems strange to me," said the Scotchman.

"Oh, no. Schinkelwitz is a very common name. Most peoples admire my name."

Tom was considerably amused, but Herr Schinkelwitz did not observe the smile which he could not repress.

"I have told my friends you would like to sell out the business," said Miles.

"Oh, ja, it is a good business, but my health is not good. I think it will be much better at the mines. You will do well to buy it yourself."

"I would if I had money enough."

"Ja, I must have the money, for I shall need it."

"My friend here has money, and may buy of you," said Miles, indicating Tom.

"What, the boy?"

"Yes."

"Where did he get so much money?"

"At the mines."

"Oh, ja, that is a good place to get gold. Well, my young vriend, I will sell cheap."

It will not be necessary to enter into a detailed account of the negotiation. It is enough to say that for the sum of seven hundred dollars Herr Schinkelwitz made over the business to Herr Tom, as he called him, and our hero found himself penniless, but the owner of a grocery. In half an hour it was all completed.

"Now, Tom, you are my boss," said Miles. "Shall I put your name outside?"

"No, John, put your own. I am only a silent partner, you know."

"I congratulate you, Tom," said Ferguson. "Here are two hundred dollars, for which you can give me your note."

"Two hundred?"

"Yes. You will need some yourself, besides what you send to your father."

"Suppose I can't pay you back?"

"Then I will levy on the grocery, my lad," said Ferguson.

CHAPTER XXII

A GAMBLING HOUSE

Having completed this important business arrangement, the two friends went out to explore the town. The limits were narrow compared with those of the flourishing city of the present day. Where the Palace and Grand hotels now stand was a sand-hill, and the bay encroached upon the business part of the city far more than now.

Scarcely a stone's throw from the grocery, on Montgomery street, between California and Sacramento, was the office of Adams' Express, which advertised to forward gold dust and packages by every steamer.

"I will go in here, Mr. Ferguson," said Tom. "I shall not feel comfortable till I have started this money homeward. I am sure it will be wanted."

"Right, my lad. We will attend to it, by all means."

They entered the building--a very humble one it would now be considered--but they found other customers before them and had to wait for their turn.

"What can I do for you?" asked the clerk, in a quick, business-like tone.

"I want to send home a hundred dollars," said Tom.

"Give me the address."

This was done, the money paid over, and a receipt returned in two minutes.

"How long before my father will receive the money?" asked Tom.

"The steamer starts in three days. About a month will be needed."

Then Tom moved aside, and the next man took his place.

"I am glad that is attended to," said Tom, relieved. "Now, Mr. Ferguson, I will go wherever you wish."

"We had better secure a lodging," said the Scotchman. "When we are sure of a bed we can walk about at our leisure."

Lodgings were to be had, but they were generally very dear. The first room looked at was five dollars per day, without board--a price our friends were unwilling to pay. Finally they found a decent, though small room, with rather a narrow bed, which could be had for three fifths of that sum, and they took it.

"We will have to go back to the mines soon," said Tom. "San Francisco is too expensive for us to live in."

"You can afford it better than I, Tom," said his friend.

"Why?"

"Because you have a business that brings you an income."

"Oh, I forgot that," said our hero, smiling. "Things happen so fast here that I haven't got used to my new position. Do you think I invested my money wisely, Mr. Ferguson?"

"Yes, my lad, since your agent is a trustworthy, honest man."

"I am sure I can trust John Miles."

"If I were not confident of it, also, I would not have encouraged you to take so important a step."

"I think I won't write to father about it," said Tom, after a pause. "He might think I had acted foolishl and become anxious. If I succeed, then I shall be glad to surprise him. I think I shall make money, but I don't want to count on it too much. I shall be ready to go back with you to the mines whenever you say the word."

As they sauntered about, gazing curiously at the motley sights around them, they heard strains of music. It appeared to proceed from a large wooden building, with a jutting roof, under which, on benches, lounged a number of persons, some of them Mexicans, in their native costumes, smoking cigarettes. A large American flag was displayed over the door, and a crowd was constantly passing in and out.

"Let us go in," said Tom.

His companion made no objection, and they entered. The first sight of the interior made clear the character of the place. There were numerous tables, spread with games--faro, monte, and roulette--each surrounded by an absorbed and interested group. "Easy come, easy go," was the rule with the early California pioneers, and the gaming-table enlisted in its service many men who would not have dreamed at home that they could ever be brought to tolerate such an instrument of evil.

Tom was a country boy, and unsophisticated, but he could not help understanding the nature of the business which brought so many to the place.

"I suppose they are gambling," he said.

"Yes, poor, deluded creatures!" said the Scotchman, who had been brought up to an abhorrence of games of chance. "They are wasting their time and their substance and foolishly laying up for themselves future misery."

Had this remark been heard it would have excited indignation, and perhaps subjected the speaker to insult, but the players were too intent upon their varying chances to pay any attention to the remarks of by-standers.

"I hope, Tom, you will never yield to the seductive lures of the gaming-table," continued Ferguson.

"I don't think there is much danger," said Tom. "I have always been taught that gambling is wicked."

"May you long feel so, my lad!"

Tom did, however, watch the players with interest. He saw money lost and won, without understanding exactly how it was decided. From the game his attention was drawn to the gamesters. He was led to notice, particularly, a young man of prepossessing countenance, who was evidently profoundly excited. From time to time he drew out a roll of gold pieces, which he placed on a card and invariably lost. He must have had a considerable sum, but, small or large, he was in ill-luck, and he constantly lost. As he neared the end of his resources the feverish blush upon his handsome features was succeeded by a deep pallor, and there was no mistaking the expression of deep anguish and despair which announced that he had reached the end.

A man loses his last cent in a gambling house, 1849

Tom became painfully interested in the young man and silently drew the attention of his companion to him. When the end came, and the victim, thoroughly "cleaned out," turned to go out, Tom said, in a low voice, "Let us follow him."

Ferguson acquiesced. He, too, had become interested, and the young man's expression as he passed our two friends was so despairing that Ferguson felt some alarm as to the effect of his disappointment upon his mind.

Once in the street, Ferguson and Tom followed the unfortunate young man into an obscure street, keeping up with difficulty, for his pace was rapid and excited. It proved to be a fortunate thing, for when he supposed himself free from observation the young man drew a pistol, and, with an incoherent exclamation, placed it in contact with his temple.

Tom sprang forward, and so did the Scotchman, but Tom was the quicker and more agile, and he dashed the pistol aside just in time to prevent a suicide.

"Why did you do that?" asked the baffled would-be-suicide, gloomily, turning his gaze upon Tom.

"I was afraid you were going to kill yourself."

"So I was."

"What could induce you to take such a rash step?" asked Ferguson.

"I have been a reckless fool. I have lost all my money at the accursed gambling-table, and my life is not worth retaining."

"It appears to me," said the Scotchman, quietly, "that you set too high a value upon money. You have certainly been very foolish to risk it at the gaming-table, and the loss will no doubt inconvenience you, but was your money all you had to live for?"

The young man regarded Ferguson with some surprise, but his excitement was evidently abated. The quiet tone of the speaker had a favorable effect upon him.

"I didn't think of it in that light," he admitted.

"Have you no relatives to whom your life is of value?"

"Yes," answered the young man. "I have a mother and sister."

"Would not your death affect them more than the loss of money?"

"Yes."

"It seems to me that to take your life would be to treat them cruelly."

The young man was evidently agitated by contending thoughts.

"I suppose you are right," he said, slowly, "but let me tell you all, and you can judge me better. I arrived in California six months ago. My home is in Ohio, not far from Cincinnati. I was fortunate enough to commence mining at a point on the western slope of the Sierra Nevada Mountains where I was almost alone. I 'struck it rich,' and two days since arrived in San Francisco with over two thousand dollars in gold dust."

"You were certainly in luck," said Ferguson, surprised.

"I turned it into money, and, in strolling about the city, was lured into that accursed den. I looked on and was fascinated. I thought I would try my luck. I began with a small stake and kept on till I had lost every dollar. In one hour the fruits of six months' labor are gone. Do you wonder that I am reduced to despair?"

CHAPTER XXIII

A NEW SCHEME

"I see no cause for despair," replied Ferguson, in the same calm tone.

"I have not a penny left out of the two thousand dollars I had only an hour ago."

"I understand all that."

"I am a ruined man," said the young man, despondently.

"I don't admit that. How old are you?"

"Twenty-one."

"You are well and strong, are you not?"

"Oh, yes, I have nothing to complain of on that score."

"Then it appears to me that your loss is not serious. Your capital still remains."

"My capital?" repeated the young man.

"Yes, your strong arms, your education, your capacity to labor."

"But I shall have to begin over again."

"Beginning over again at your age, when, possibly, fifty years of life lie before you, is not such a serious matter. Were I in your situation--and I am twice as old as you--I should not think of despairing. Don't you think it would be rather foolish for two thousand dollars, which you have been only six months in accumulating, to throw away fifty years, and all that you can make in that time, thereby bringing a lifelong grief to your mother and sister?"

The calm, logical tone of the Scotchman had its effect.

"I see that I was about to add to one piece of folly another far greater," said the young man. "I don't know who you are, sir, but I heartily thank you and your son for saving my life."

"This is not my son, but my young friend, Thomas Nelson," said Ferguson. "I am not so fortunate as to have a son."

"Well, God bless you both, and good night!"

"Excuse my persistency, but may I ask where you are going?"

"I am not going to repeat my folly of just now, if that is what you mean."

"I did not suspect you of that, but are you sure of a bed anywhere?"

"No, I have no money to pay for one. I shall walk the streets or possibly lie down in some quiet place. I was accustomed to roughing it at the mines and can do it again if necessary."

"Tom and I have a room in which you are welcome to find a shelter. I am sorry that our bed is too narrow to hold another."

"Thank you. That will be better than to sleep in the streets. But are you not afraid to make me this offer?"

"Why should I be?"

"I might rob you during the night."

"You might, but you don't look like one who would so reward confidence."

"You are right. If you had fifty thousand dollars I would not touch a dollar of it. I will accept your offer. How can I repay you for your kindness?"

"There may be a way. We will talk of that this evening."

Nine o'clock found the three collected in the small room which had been hired by Ferguson for himself and Tom.

"My friend," said Ferguson, "you told us that you found a favorable place for mining up in the Sierras."

"Yes, I 'struck it rich.'"

"I take it for granted that you did not exhaust the wealth of the place?"

"Far from it. I only dipped into it. There is abundance left."

"Is this place known to many?"

"To only one, so far as I know. He and I worked independently but were company for each other."

"But what induced you to leave so rich a claim?"

"I was tired of working and wanted to come to the city for a change. You know what a change I have experienced here."

"Why don't you go back and start anew in the place where you met with your former good fortune?" asked Ferguson.

"Because I am penniless. I must find something to do here for a while. When I have got together a little fund, sufficient for the purpose, I will go back."

"Would you go back now, if you had the chance?"

"Would I? Certainly I would, for I could make money faster there than here."

"Would you have any objection to let Tom and myself accompany you?"

"Not the least. I should be glad of your company. There is gold enough for us all."

"Then we will start tomorrow, that is, if you and Tom are willing."

"I am ready," said Tom, promptly.

"But I have nothing. I don't like to be an expense to you," objected the young man.

"We will pay your expenses. We shall be more than recompensed by the richness of the mines. We might find something to do here, but both Tom and myself prefer the freedom of the mining camp, and, if the spot is as rich as you have led us to suspect, we shall make more money there."

"Agreed!" said the young man, promptly. "Name the hour of starting, and rely upon me to be ready."

Ferguson was evidently well pleased with this response. He felt that his new acquaintance would be so far away from the city and would sooner retrieve his fortunes at the mines. He hoped, too, to find opportunity to strengthen his principles and guard him against the temptations of the city when he should again visit it. Again, he had reason to think that the arrangement would benefit Tom and himself in a pecuniary way, and the Scotchman was by no means indifferent to that consideration, though, as we have seen, he did not unduly exalt the power or value of money.

Tom, too, was pleased with the prospect. He was grateful and attached to Ferguson, whom he felt to be a true friend, but he was glad to have another companion nearer his own age. The young man was of a prepossessing exterior, and, when he had shaken off his present disquietude, looked as if he might be a cheerful and agreeable companion.

"Since we are to live together, for a time at least, and become fellow workers," said Ferguson, "we ought to know each other better. I will introduce myself first."

Hereupon Ferguson gave a brief account of himself, which need not be repeated, and then called upon Tom, who followed his example.

"Now it is my turn," said their new acquaintance. "You don't even know my name yet, though you have done me such an important service. I have already told you that I am from Ohio. My name is Richard Russell, though my friends generally call me Dick. My father, whom I had the misfortune to lose several years ago, was at one time a member of Congress. He left a small property, the income of which is barely sufficient to provide my mother and sister with the comforts of life. I had a fair education, including enough Latin and Greek to fit me for entering college. My mother desired me to enter, but I knew that she could not keep me there without practicing pinching economy, and I secured a place with a small salary in a business house in Cincinnati. A year since, when the papers were full of the gold discoveries on this coast, I was seized, like so many others, with the golden fever, and I arranged to start overland. It would have proved a wise step had I not been so rash a fool as to squander my earnings, for two thousand dollars in six months compare very favorably with twelve dollars a week, which I was earning at home. I might have gone home by the next steamer, and I had money enough to carry me through a course of legal study, had I desired. I am out of patience with myself when I think of how I have thrown away my good fortune."

"Don't think too much of the past, which cannot be recalled. Resolve not to repeat your folly, and all may yet be well."

"I have fully resolved upon that," said Russell, earnestly.

"Do you think you shall study law, if you are again fortunate, Mr. Russell?" asked Tom.

"If you please don't call me Mr. Russell, unless you want me to call you Mr. Nelson. Call me Dick."

"I will," said Tom, smiling, "for I am not ready to be called Mr. Nelson yet."

"Now, to answer your question. If I can get two thousand dollars together again, I shall probably study law. Of course I don't mean to be a miner all my life any more than you. Now, Tom, what are your plans?"

"I think I should like to be a lawyer, too, but I must earn more than two thousand dollars first."

"Two thousand ought to be sufficient to educate you if you are economical."

"It would be, but I want to pay off a mortgage on my father's farm before I begin to lay up money for myself."

"You are a good fellow, Tom, and I wish you success."

"Thank you, Dick. I will succeed if hard work can bring success."

"Good night to you both," said Ferguson. "I want to sleep well to prepare myself for starting tomorrow."

In half an hour all three were sleeping soundly.

CHAPTER XXIV

PREPARING FOR A NEW START

When Tom opened his eyes he did not at first remember where he was, but a glance at Dick Russell, his new acquaintance, stretched out on the floor and still sleeping, quickly recalled the important events of the day previous. Mr. Ferguson was already dressed.

"Well, Tom, are you rested?" he asked.

"Yes, Mr. Ferguson. I slept like a top. What time is it?"

"It is seven o'clock. Our new friend is still asleep."

"I suppose he was on his feet all day yesterday."

"I don't know whether I ought to hurry you away from San Francisco so soon, Tom," said his Scotch friend. "We only arrived yesterday, and you have not had time to see the place and enjoy yourself after your hard work at the mines."

"I don't care for that, Mr. Ferguson. I am anxious to be at work again. I didn't come out here to enjoy myself but to make money for my father."

"You have succeeded pretty well thus far, Tom."

"Yes, but I have made more by the sale of the team than by work at the mines."

Seeking gold in California: Tom and Mr. Ferguson reflect back on River Bend and on the new start that awaits them.

"True, but that is a legitimate transaction. If our friend here has reported correctly, we shall find mining more profitable in the place he mentions than at River Bend."

"I have no objection to that, though I was satisfied with River Bend. Wouldn't it be splendid, Mr. Ferguson, if we could do as well in the next six months as he did?"

"Making two thousand dollars each?"

"Yes."

"We may accomplish it, but it is best not to calculate upon it."

"If I could only free the farm from that troublesome mortgage I should be proud and happy. It has worn upon father, as I could see, and he has been compelled to toil early and late to pay the interest, besides supporting us all."

"How much is the mortgage, Tom?"

"Twenty-two hundred dollars."

"You have made a good beginning towards it already, Tom. You have seven hundred dollars invested in business."

"But out of that I owe you a hundred and fifty, Mr. Ferguson."

"Don't trouble yourself about that, Tom. Unless I should stand in great need of it, I will wait till you have paid off the mortgage before asking to have it repaid."

"You are very kind, Mr. Ferguson," said Tom, gratefully. "A part of my seven hundred dollars rightfully belongs to you, for you owned two-thirds of the horse and wagon."

"I couldn't have bought them without your help, Tom. So you see that you enabled me to make money. I am quite satisfied with an equal partnership."

"And I am very well satisfied with my partner," said Tom, smiling. "Shall we wake up Russell?"

"Yes, for we have much to do today."

"John Miles will be surprised at my leaving the city so quick."

"By the way, Tom, as he is to remain here, while you are out of the reach of post-offices, it may be well to ask your father to direct future letters to his care, and he can forward them as he has opportunity."

"That is a good idea. I will write today so as to catch the next steamer, and I will also speak to John."

Tom had to shake Dick Russell energetically before that young man opened his eyes.

"What's the matter?" he cried, drowsily.

"Don't you want some breakfast?" asked Tom.

"Oh, it's you, Tom! Yes, you have touched the right chord. I have a first-class appetite--and no money," he added, his face clouding.

"Mr. Ferguson is treasurer," said Tom, lightly, wishing to divert Russell from the thoughts of his heavy loss and the folly to which he owed it, "but we know very little of the city. Can you guide us to a good restaurant?"

"To a good one, but not a cheap one. Everything is high here."

"Then it is fortunate we are going to leave so soon."

In a small restaurant on Montgomery street, our three friends partook of a hearty breakfast. It might not have attracted an epicure, but neither of the three was fastidious, and, though the charge was five dollars, Ferguson, economical as he was, paid the bill cheerfully. It was the first "civilized" breakfast he had eaten for months, and it might be months before he would be able to partake of another as good.

"I wish we could breakfast like this at the mines," said Tom.

"So say I," chimed in Dick Russell, "but you know that the gold-hunter must sacrifice home comforts."

"I shan't complain of that, if I can do as well as you did," said Tom.

"I see no reason why you can't. There is plenty of gold there, and all that is needed is work and perseverance."

"I am willing to contribute them," said Tom. "I mean to do my best to succeed."

"None of us can do more, my lad," said Ferguson. "Let us hope that God will prosper our undertakings."

"I say, I am glad I have met with you two," said Dick Russell. "You'll keep me on the right track, and, in spite of my past folly, I hope in time to win success."

"I am glad to hear you speak so sensibly, my young friend," said the Scotchman, kindly. "It's a great deal better to put your back to the wheel once more than to take the life God gave you."

"Don't speak of that again, Mr. Ferguson," said Russell, shuddering. "I don't like to think of it."

"He'll do," thought Ferguson, with satisfaction. "His mind is now in a healthy condition, and I have great hopes for him."

The rest of the day was devoted to the purchase of supplies. Ferguson also bought a mule, on behalf of the party, which was of service in carrying a part of their burdens. It was not until afternoon that Tom found an opportunity to call on John Miles and acquaint him with his almost immediate departure.

"I am sorry you are going away so soon, Tom," said Miles. "I thought you would stay at least a week."

"So I would if I were not so anxious to be at work once more. You know how my father is situated, John, for I have told you more than once."

"Yes, Tom, but I see no reason why you should feel uneasy. With the help you are to send him, there will be no trouble about his paying his interest regularly."

"I know that, John, but I shall feel uneasy until the mortgage is paid off and he is out of Squire Hudson's power."

"For how long a time has the farm your father owns been encumbered with this mortgage?"

"For ten years, at least."

"Is the mortgage for any specified term of years?"

"I don't think so."

"It merely runs from year to year then?"

"I suppose so."

"In that case this Squire Hudson could foreclose at any time, could he not?"

"Yes," answered Tom, soberly.

"Don't make yourself uneasy about it, however," said Miles, observing that Tom seemed apprehensive. "As your father's farm is not particularly valuable, there can be no danger of foreclosure. By the way, wouldn't you like to have me remit your father something next month out of the profits of the business? I can charge it to your account."

"I am glad you mentioned it, John. You may send him fifty or seventy-five dollars, if my share should amount to so much."

"I will."

"And I am going to have my home letters directed to your care. You can forward them to me whenever you have an opportunity."

"I won't fail, Tom. If there is anything you need sent out to you, you have only to write me, and I will attend to your commissions."

"It is very convenient to have an agent in the city," said Tom, smiling. "I shall feel much more comfortable out at the mines."

"I wish you good luck, Tom, but remember, even if you don't succeed in your search for gold, I shall be making money for you here."

"You make me feel quite like a capitalist, John."

"I hope you may be one some day. Good bye!"

They shook hands and parted. Before nightfall Tom had started on his new journey in quest of gold.

CHAPTER XXV

WHITEFACE

Mark Nelson missed sorely the cow which he had been compelled to yield to the squire on account of default of interest. Whiteface was his best cow and a great favorite with all the children. She gave nearly as much milk as the other two and had been one of the main dependences of the family. It was worth considerably more than the thirty dollars for which the squire took it, but he insisted upon that and no other, and Whiteface had to go.

Six months had passed, and there seemed to be very little chance of redeeming the lost cow. Squire Hudson had agreed to give her back on payment of the balance due, with accrued interest, but neither he nor Mark Nelson expected that such an offer would be made.

"I was passing Squire Hudson's today and saw poor Whiteface," said Walter one evening. "I think she knew me, for when I called her she lowed back."

"I wish we had her back," said Sarah. "It was heartless of the squire to take her. He has a dozen cows of his own."

"He hasn't any heart," said Walter, "or, if he has, it must be pretty small."

"We must not forget that he was entitled to some security for the balance of interest I owe him," said the farmer.

"The cow was worth a good deal more than thirty dollars," said Sarah.

"Yes, she was, but I am not sure whether I could have got any more money for her at a forced sale. Then you know the squire is pledged to give her back whenever I can pay him the thirty dollars, with interest."

"I wish you could pay it now, father," said Walter.

"So do I, my boy, but I cannot, unless your brother sends me some money."

"It is three weeks since we have heard from Tom," said Mrs. Nelson, anxiously. "I am afraid he is sick."

"Don't worry yourself with imaginary fears, Mary," said her husband. "Tom may be sick, of course, but he is strong and healthy, and we won't fear such a thing without some ground. Probably a letter is on the way from him now."

"I hope he is making money," said Walter. "I wish I were with him."

"I would never consent to have you go too," said Mrs. Nelson, hastily.

"I don't think Walter seriously thinks of leaving," said Mr. Nelson, smiling. "As he is only thirteen years old, I should be inclined to object myself. I must have him at home to help me with the farm."

"I should be perfectly contented to stay at home if we had Whiteface back," said Walter. "I've a great mind to steal her out of the squire's yard. I bet she'd be glad to come."

"Don't speak in that way, Walter," said his father. "I dislike to have you speak of stealing, even in fun."

At this moment there was a knock at the front door. Farmer Nelson's house was an old-fashioned one, and it was not provided with a bell.

"Go to the door, Sarah," said her father.

Sarah obeyed.

"Good evening, Nahum," she said to the village expressman.

"I've got a small package for your folks," said Nahum. "It's marked all over. Guess it came from Californy."

"It must be from Tom," exclaimed Sarah, in delight.

"That's what I thought," said the expressman, who knew everybody in the village and could probably give a fairly correct list of their sisters, cousins, and aunts, with a fair guess at their worldly circumstances.

"Is there anything to pay, Nahum?"

"Only fifty cents--the expressage from Boston. Never mind about it now, for I'm in a hurry. Your father can hand it to me next time he sees me."

"Oh father, here's a package from Tom," said Sarah, hurrying into the room where they were all sitting.

"Open it quick," said Walter. "See if there's any money in it."

The cord was cut, and a small box was disclosed containing a hundred dollars in gold pieces and a line from Tom, stating that he was doing well and that he hoped soon to send some more money.

"A hundred dollars! What a lot of money!" exclaimed Walter, gazing on the little pile of coins as if fascinated.

"I am so glad the dear boy is doing well," said Mrs. Nelson.

"Now we can have Whiteface back, can't we, father?" asked Walter, joyfully.

"Yes, Walter," said Mark Nelson, almost as excited as his son. "I will go over the first thing in the morning."

"Can't we go over this evening?" asked Walter, impatiently.

"No, it is dark, and Whiteface is stalled for the night."

"You'll have seventy dollars left over, father, won't you?"

"Yes, and that will provide for my next interest. I feel grateful and happy at Tom's success and his thoughtfulness."

Could Tom have seen the effect of his remittance it would have made his heart glad, and he would have felt abundantly repaid for his labor and self-denial.

CHAPTER XXVI

SQUIRE HUDSON'S DISAPPOINTMENT

If Whiteface was missed at her old home, she was scarcely less appreciated by her new possessor. On the very morning succeeding the day when Tom's remittance was received, the squire remarked to his head workman, "Whiteface is an excellent cow, Abner."

"Yes, squire, I calculate she's the best you've got."

"I don't know but she is, Abner," said the squire, complacently. "I consider her worth at least fifty dollars."

"So she is, every cent of it."

"And she cost me only thirty," thought Squire Hudson, with a smile of content.

He was a rich man and abundantly able to pay his poor neighbor the full value of the cow, but somehow it never occurred to him to do it. He was not above taking an unfair advantage of a man who was unluckily in his power. Of course the squire knew that Farmer Nelson had a right to redeem the cow at the price agreed upon with interest, but he felt pretty safe on this point. The farmer was not very likely to have thirty dollars to spare, and as for a remittance from Tom the squire was pretty sure none would be received.

"It'll be all the boy can do to take care of himself out there," he reflected, "let alone sending money home. He may send ten dollars or so some time, but it's very doubtful, very doubtful!"

Squire Hudson turned to go back to the house when he saw the man of whom he had been thinking coming up the road. He stopped short, thinking the farmer might wish to speak to him.

"Good morning, Mr. Nelson," he said, pleasantly, for he was in good-humor.

"Good morning, squire."

"Your Whiteface has got to feel quite at home in my barnyard."

"She is a good cow, Squire Hudson."

"Yes, tolerable, tolerable."

"She is worth more than the thirty dollars for which you took her."

118

"Well, I don't know about that. Cows are pretty cheap nowadays."

"I see how it is," thought the squire. "Nelson wants me to allow him more for the cow, but a bargain is a bargain, and I shan't do it."

"I always valued her at a considerably higher price."

"No doubt, no doubt. You raised her yourself, didn't you?"

"Yes."

"That makes a difference, of course. You attach a sentimental value to her, but that doesn't affect her real value. I really can't allow you any more for her."

"I don't want you to, Squire Hudson."

The squire looked astonished.

"What is the man driving at?" he thought.

"She may not be worth any more to you, and so you won't mind my taking her back."

"Taking her back!" exclaimed the squire.

"Certainly, it was agreed that I could redeem her at any time by paying you the thirty dollars and interest."

"Not after two months," said the squire, hastily.

"It is not two months. It was only six weeks yesterday. The fact is, squire, I've come for Whiteface, and I've got the money for you."

"Have you heard from Tom?" asked the squire, with a blank look of disappointment.

"Yes, I heard from him yesterday."

"And he sent you some money?"

"Yes, he reports that he is doing well."

"Did he send you thirty dollars?"

"Rather more than that," said Mark Nelson, not caring to gratify the curiosity of his creditor.

"I think you had better keep your money and leave Whiteface with me," said Squire Hudson, after a pause.

"I would rather not, squire. The fact is, Whiteface is a sort of pet at home, and we all want her back."

Squire Hudson was disconcerted. He had not expected that Mr. Nelson would be able to redeem the cow, and he was reluctant to give her up. But there was no excuse for retaining her. His agreement stood in the way.

"Neighbor Nelson," he said, after a pause, "I don't mind giving you five dollars over and above what you owe me for Whiteface. Come, that's a good offer."

Mark Nelson shook his head.

"She's worth more than that," he said. "But that's neither here nor there. I raised the animal, and it was sorely against my will that I parted with her six weeks ago. Now that I have the money to pay you, I want her back."

"I think you are standing in your own light, Mr. Nelson," said the squire. "I have taken a fancy to the cow and am willing to pay more for her than she is worth. I will say ten dollars."

Mark Nelson shook his head.

"I'd rather have Whiteface than the money," he said.

"If she comes into my possession again," said Squire Hudson, "I shall not be willing to grant you the privilege of redeeming her. It won't be many months before another payment becomes due."

"I hope to be ready to meet it, squire," said the farmer, not appearing at all anxious.

Mark Nelson's favorite cow, Whiteface

"He seems very independent," thought the squire, watching, moodily, the cow driven away by her former owner. "He may sing another tune on interest day. I wonder how much the boy sent home."

Had he known that Mr. Nelson had in his pocket enough money to pay the whole of the next accruing interest, he would have felt more doubtful about recovering the cow which he now coveted more than ever.

"Well, Abner, I've lost her," said the squire, hurrying to his assistant, "but she'll be back here some day, mark my words!"

"I thought you bought her, squire," said Abner, in surprise.

"Well, not exactly. I took her for a debt, but Nelson had the right of redeeming her, and he has done it. His boy sent him the money."

"That Tom Nelson is a smart boy," said Abner, who, though in the squire's employ, was friendly to our hero.

"Well, so-so," remarked the squire, indifferently. "I helped him to go to California, but I am not sure whether it was a wise step. I let my feelings get the better of my judgment."

"Then it is the first time," was Abner's unspoken comment.

"It may turn out for the best," he said aloud.

"I doubt if I shall ever see my money again," said the squire, but he did not seem to take it to heart, judging from his manner and tone.

"Didn't you have security for the loan?" asked Abner.

"Well, ye-es," answered the squire, slowly, "but not very good. The farm was already mortgaged for its full value."

"The squire is getting benevolent," thought Abner, "or he wants me to think so, but I'm inclined to think he has some object under it all. What is it?"

A few weeks later Farmer Nelson's heart was gladdened by the receipt of another remittance, this time sent by John Miles, out of the profit of the business in which Tom was his partner. The amount this time was seventy-five dollars. It made him feel quite rich.

"Mary," he said, "we all need some new clothes, and I propose to use this money for that purpose. Now I want you to consider how we can spend it to the best advantage. To begin with, you must buy a new dress. You have long needed one."

Mrs. Nelson demurred a little but was forced to admit that the dress was needed. So the purchases were made at once. It is wonderful how far seventy-five dollars will go in an economical family of plain tastes. It was soon apparent to the neighbors that the Nelsons were exhibiting signs of prosperity.

"It must be Tom," they decided.

Efforts were made to ascertain just how much our hero had sent home, but on this point the Nelsons would not speak definitely. They reported in general terms that Tom was doing well.

Of course Squire Hudson was not ignorant of the apparent improvement in the fortunes of his debtor. Strange to say, he seemed rather annoyed. He was pleased, however, by the outlay for dress.

"They're getting extravagant, Abner," he said, cheerfully. "I thought Mark Nelson was a man of more sense. Because his son has sent home a little money, he must rig out the whole family in new clothes. 'A fool and his money are soon parted.'"

"Mark Nelson is no fool," said Abner, stoutly.

"He is in this instance," said the squire, sharply. "However, I don't object to it, if he likes to violate the rules of prudence. It strikes me, however, that it would be well for him to pay up the money I advanced for Tom's expenses, before buying new clothes wholesale."

Abner repeated this to Mr. Nelson.

The farmer answered quietly, "The squire is not wholly wrong. It is good doctrine to pay your debts before you spend money for what you don't need. In this case, however, we did need the clothes we bought. Now that we are provided, I hope, before very long, if Tom is prospered, to pay back the two hundred dollars the squire advanced for him."

"I hope you will, I'm sure," said Abner. "That's a smart boy of yours, and I always said so."

"He is a good boy, and I am sure he will do what is right."

"He's a blamed sight better than the squire's boy. Sinclair is a stuck-up jackanapes, and it would do me good to kick him."

"It might not do him any good."

"I am not sure about that. I think he needs it."

CHAPTER XXVII

THE NEW DIGGINGS

Meanwhile Tom and his party, pursuing their journey by easy stages, for they sensibly determined not to overtask their strength, reached at last the spot of which Russell had spoken. Ferguson and Tom soon found that he had not exaggerated. The new diggings were certainly far richer than those at River Bend. It was, in fact, the bed of a dead river upon which Russell had stumbled without knowing it. My readers are probably aware that in the beds of rivers or creeks the early miners found their first harvest of gold, and, that, where practicable, these were mined by turning the stream in the dry season, when the water was low. As it may not be so well understood what is meant by a dead river, I quote a passage from an article in the "Overland Monthly," as found in the pages of the "Pacific Coast Mining Review," for the year 1878-79:

"A dead river is one which formerly existed, but exists no longer. In volcanic regions it sometimes happens that the liquid lava, seeking the lowest ground, fills up the beds of the rivers which die and are replaced by water-courses running in other channels and in different directions. These dead streams are so few, and of so little importance elsewhere, that, as yet, I believe, no class name has been given to them; but in California they are among the chief source of its mineral wealth, and among the most remarkable features of its geological formation. They take us back to a remote era, before the time of Rome, of Greece, or of Egypt; far back beyond the origin of history or tradition, before our coast had taken its present shapes; before Shasta, and Lassen, and Castle Peaks had poured out their lava floods; before the Sacramento river had its birth; and while, if not before, the mastodon, the elephant, the rhinoceros, the horse, the mammoth bull, the tapir, and the bison lived in the land. They are indeed among the most remarkable discoveries of the age, and among the greatest wonders of geology. They deserve some common name, and we have to choose between 'extinct' and 'dead.' We speak of 'extinct volcanoes,' and of 'dead languages,' and, as the latter is Saxon and short, we prefer it. They have been called 'old channels;' but this name does not convey the proper idea, since a channel is not necessarily a river, and an old channel is not necessarily a dead one. A dead river is a channel formerly occupied by a running stream, but now filled up with earthy or rocky matter, and is not to be confounded with a channel that is open and remains dry during the greater part of the year because of a lack of water, or that has been abandoned by the stream for a deeper channel elsewhere. A dry river-bed is not a dead river.

"The dead rivers of California, so far as are known, are on the western slope of the Sierra Nevada, from five hundred to seven thousand feet above the level of the sea. They are all gold-yielding, and therefore they have been sought and examined. They have yielded probably three hundred millions in all; they now produce perhaps eight million dollars annually. They are not less interesting to the miner than to the geologist, not less important to the statesman than to the antiquarian."

At the risk of being considered tedious by some of my readers, I will transcribe the writer's explanation of the existence of these dead rivers. For this reason we must go back to a remote geological epoch: "The main cause must have been the subsequent rise of the Sierra Nevada. Suppose that a range of mountains, seven thousand feet high, were upheaved thirty miles east of the Mississippi; that the bed of that stream were on the mountain side, three thousand feet above the sea, and that thirty miles west the country maintained its present level; the result would be that the present Mississippi would soon be a dead river; it would be cut across by streams running down the mountain side, and flowing into a new Mississippi, thirty miles or more west of the present one. We know that the Sierra Nevada has been upheaved; that a large stream ran on what is now the mountain side, and that it has been succeeded by a new river farther west, and we must infer that the death of the old and the birth of the new river were caused by the upheaval."

Reference is here made to the Big Blue Lead, the largest dead river known in California, which has been traced for a distance of sixty-five miles, from Little Grizzly, in Sierra County, to Forest Hill, in Placer County. The original river, however, is thought to have run for many hundreds of miles. Eventually traces of its existence may be found elsewhere.

It is not to be supposed that Tom and his friends knew anything about dead rivers, or troubled themselves as to how the rich deposits had been made, or how long they had been waiting discovery. They were chiefly engaged with more practical considerations. They found a rich harvest in the ravines, and they went to work energetically.

The work was monotonous, and a detailed account of their progress would be tiresome. What we chiefly care about is results, and these may be gathered from a conversation which took place some five months later.

Under a tent, at nightfall, reclined the three friends. They looked contented and on good terms with the world, but, though prosperous, they certainly did not look it. In fact, they were all three exceedingly, almost disreputably, shabby. They looked more like tramps than respectable gold miners.

"Tom, you are looking very ragged," said Dick Russell, surveying our hero critically.

"I know it, Dick. I feel as though I had just come out of a rag-bag. I can't say that you look much better, nor Ferguson either."

"This rough work is hard on clothing," said Russell. "I wish there were a ready-made clothing store near by."

"So do I. I would pay a high price for a good suit."

"If our friends at home could see us, what would they think, eh, Tom?"

"That we were candidates for the poorhouse."

"That's so. I've been into several poorhouses in the course of my life, but I never saw any of the inmates quite so poorly clad as we are."

"You are right," said Ferguson, "but there are generally compensations. I was taking account of stock, and I estimate that I have from sixteen to eighteen hundred dollars' worth of gold dust."

"I have nearly as much," said Tom.

"My pile won't vary far from Tom's," said Russell.

"That is a pretty good showing for five months, my friend," said the Scotchman.

"It will make up for the old clothes," said Tom.

"I have been thinking," said Ferguson, "that we need a vacation. What do you say to starting next week for San Francisco?"

"I agree," said Russell, promptly.

"And I," said Tom. "I should like to see John Miles."

"Very well. We will continue our work about a week longer and then start."

CHAPTER XXVIII

A RICH DEPOSIT

About the middle of the next morning Tom suddenly stopped work.

"What's the matter, Tom? Are you tired?"

"No, but I feel like exploring a little. Who goes with me?"

"Not I," answered Ferguson. "Let well enough alone."

"I'll go with you," said Russell. "I should like a holiday. Besides, we may discover something."

"'A rolling stone gathers no moss,'" said Ferguson.

"True, but there's another proverb: 'All work and no play makes Jack a dull boy.' Tom and I will try a little play."

The two friends sauntered away in an idle mood, yet, combining business with pleasure, they watched carefully the surface indications, ready to avail themselves of any that were favorable.

"It's a strange life we are leading, Tom," said Russell. "It is free, and independent, and healthful, but I shouldn't like to live so all my life."

"Nor I," answered Tom. "No amount of gold would repay me."

"Because gold is only valuable for what it will bring. Here it brings nothing."

"Except the hope of future ease and comfort," suggested Tom.

"Of course, that is what we are working for. We have made a good beginning."

"Yes, Dick. I have almost accomplished what I have had in view ever since I left home."

"I know. You mean paying off your father's mortgage."

"That's it. It amounts to twenty-two hundred dollars, and I have but a few hundred dollars more to earn. I would stay here a month or two longer, if my clothes would hold together, but I can't risk it."

"You need rest, at any rate, Tom, leaving clothes out of the question."

As he spoke, Tom, without special thought, drove his pick into the ground. It was a lucky inspiration. Some shining particles attracted the attention of Russell.

"Tom," he exclaimed, in excitement, "do you see that, and that? I believe you've struck a bonanza."

126

Upon that both set to work in earnest. A further investigation showed that Russell was right. Tom, by good luck, had chanced upon a deposit of far greater richness than any they had yet encountered.

"If it holds out, our fortunes are made, Tom," said Russell. "Go and call Ferguson, and I will remain on guard till you come back."

Tom stood not on the order of his going but went at once.

"What's the matter, Tom?" asked the Scotchman, as, panting and breathless, Tom stood before him. "Has anything happened to Russell?"

"No, it's good news--splendid news, Mr. Ferguson. We've found a place ten times as rich as this. Come at once, and see."

Ferguson made preparations to accompany Tom with what seemed to our hero to be provoking deliberation. In truth the Scotchman, with his national caution, was rather skeptical as to Tom's news and did not suffer himself to become enthusiastic or excited. Tom had hard work to accommodate his impatient steps to the measured pace of his more sedate companion. When at length they reached the spot they found Russell no less impatient.

"I thought you would never come," he said.

"Tom wanted to fly," said Ferguson, "but I am too old for that. Now, what is it you have found?"

When he was shown what had been discovered he admitted that it was very promising.

"If it holds out, we shall be lucky," he said.

"It will hold out," said Russell, enthusiastically.

"It isn't well to be too confident," said Ferguson, cautiously.

"You are very cold-blooded, Mr. Ferguson," said Russell, impatiently. "Won't anything excite you?"

"What good would it do to become excited?" returned the Scotchman. "I am as ready to test the matter as you are, and I shall rejoice if your sanguine expectations are realized. Do not expect too much, however, and you will guard against possible disappointment."

But there was no disappointment awaiting them. They worked steadily for two weeks, with marvelous results. In this time they unearthed six thousand dollars' worth of gold, which by arrangement they divided equally between them, and still the gold deposit was far from being exhausted.

At the end of the fortnight they were visited by a party of capitalists from San Francisco, who were out on an exploring expedition. They recognized the richness of the new discoveries, and after some negotiation offered the three friends ten thousand dollars for their claims. One consideration decided them to accept. It was absolutely necessary for them to go to the city for clothing and other articles, of which they stood in imperative need. They closed the bargain and started on their return.

California Gold Diggers

CHAPTER XXIX

BAD NEWS FROM HOME

Arriving in the city late in the afternoon, Tom went at once to see John Miles. When the latter caught sight of Tom, in his ragged attire, he came to the natural conclusion that our hero had met with hard luck.

"Why, Tom, where did you spring from?" he exclaimed, grasping the hand of his young partner.

"I am just in from the mines."

"I suppose you are in want of money," said Miles, his voice betraying sympathy.

Tom laughed.

"How do you like my appearance, John?" he asked.

"Never mind that, Tom. I see you have had a rough time, but I have been earning money for you."

"Did you send money regularly to father?"

"Yes. I have sent him three hundred dollars in all."

"That's good," said Tom, in a tone of satisfaction. "That has made him easy. I suppose that took up about all I was entitled to?"

"No. I have as much more to your credit. I am ready to pay it to you at once."

"I see, John, you think I have not been doing well."

"You don't look very prosperous, Tom, I must acknowledge."

"Well, John, appearances are deceitful. I have been wonderfully lucky."

"I am delighted to hear it, Tom," said Miles, cordially. "How much is it now?"

"What do you say to a thousand dollars?"

"Excellent."

"Two thousand?"

"You don't mean it!"

"I won't keep you in suspense, John. I don't know exactly how much I've got, but it's over six thousand dollars!"

John Miles stared at our hero in undisguised astonishment.

"Are you sure you're quite right here?" he said, touching his forehead. "You haven't been sunstruck, have you?"

"No, John, it's all as I tell you. Let me explain how my luck came."

In a few sentences Tom made it clear to his partner that his luck was real.

"As to the three hundred dollars due me from you, John," concluded Tom, "I make you a present of it."

"But, Tom--" protested Miles.

"Let it be so, and for the future you shall pay me my share. Have you any letters for me?"

"I have three."

"Give them to me, quick. I am hungry for news from home."

Tom sat down on a keg and fairly devoured the letters, two of which were from his father. One of these gave him much to think of. I will transcribe the passages which gave Tom most concern:

"Yesterday I paid Squire Hudson his regular semi-annual interest, amounting to sixty-six dollars. Thanks to your generous remittances, I had no difficulty in making the payment. Indeed, I had two hundred dollars left over. Imagine my dismay when the squire told me he had made up his mind to call in the mortgage, having another use for the money.

"'But I can't pay it up,' said I.

"'You ought to be able to obtain the money somewhere,' he returned.

"'You are the only capitalist with whom I am acquainted,' said I. 'Since I have paid you the interest promptly, what more can you desire?'

"He insisted that he needed the money. I offered to pay him the two hundred dollars which he had advanced for your journey. He seemed surprised but repeated that he must have the whole. The upshot of it was that he gave me a formal notice of three months, as stipulated in the mortgage. At the end of that time, unless I am ready to pay the twenty-two hundred dollars, he will foreclose, and the old farm must be sold. Of course it will be sold much below its real value. Probably the squire will get it for the amount of the mortgage, and we shall be thrown upon the world, without a home. It seems hard, Tom, and very selfish, but might makes right, and Squire Hudson has the power on his side."

In a postscript Mark Nelson added, "I understand that Squire Hudson has a connection, his wife's brother, for whom he wants the farm. That explains his resolute refusal to give me time to redeem it. Of course it is too early to decide upon any plans. I must hire some tenement to move into when I have to leave here. It will be hard upon us all to give up the old farm. Walter, who has a taste for farming, and whom I look to be my successor, feels very sad. Don't let this news depress you too much, Tom. We shall not suffer. Thanks to you, I have some money ahead, and we shall not lack for comfort."

Tom looked up when he had finished reading the letter.

"John," he said, quickly, "when does the next steamer start for New York?"

"Day after tomorrow."

"Where can I engage passage?"

"Are you going home?"

"Yes, John, it is absolutely necessary. Squire Hudson is about to foreclose the mortgage on my father's farm. I must be there to stop it."

"Have you money enough?"

"Three times over. He shall be defeated in his wicked purpose, or my name isn't Tom Nelson."

Tom spoke in a quick, indignant tone, and his voice had a manly ring.

"Wait, John, let me read you the letter."

"The man's a mean rascal!" said Miles. "A rich man who will take advantage of a poor man's necessity to deprive him of his home deserves to be horsewhipped."

"I shan't attempt that," said Tom, smiling, "but I will disappoint him. He little thinks I have it in my power to defeat his plans."

That very evening Tom engaged passage to New York, and two days later he sailed out of the Golden Gate.

"I don't know how long I shall be gone, John," he said. "You need send me no remittances, for I have money enough with me. You will hear from me as soon as I have reached home and transacted my business with Squire Hudson."

"You will come out here again, Tom, won't you?"

"Yes, and before long. I have been so busily occupied making money that I have seen almost nothing of San Francisco."

Tom did not journey alone. Ferguson, having thriven beyond his expectations, decided to sail to New York, and thence to Scotland, on a visit to his relatives, though he thought it probable he should come back within a year. Dick Russell also was now in a position to study law at home and gave up the business of gold-mining forever.

131

"I owe all my present prosperity to you two," he said. "But for you I should have blown my brains out five months ago."

"We owe our prosperity to you also," said Tom. "You guided us to the mines from which we gathered a golden harvest."

"We have worked together, and been mutual helpers," said Ferguson. "God has favored us all, and to Him be the thanks!"

CHAPTER XXX

THE NIGHT BEFORE THE AUCTION

It was a sad household, that of Mark Nelson, on the day preceding the departure from the farm. There was to be an auction the next day, at which the farm-stock and farm-implements were to be sold. It was well understood that Squire Hudson was to be the buyer of the farm, and as he was not likely to have any competitor there was little hope that it would fetch more than the amount of the mortgage.

During the afternoon Mr. Nelson called on Squire Hudson to make the best terms he could at private sale.

"The farm is worth at least a thousand dollars more than the mortgage, Squire Hudson," said the farmer.

"It is worth what it will fetch, Mr. Nelson," said the squire.

"Do you mean that an article always commands its full value at auction, Squire Hudson?"

"Ahem! It brings its market value, Mr. Nelson."

"Which may be far below its intrinsic value. Suppose a diamond worth ten thousand dollars were put up at auction in our village, do you consider that it would bring a fair price?"

"Ahem! You are wandering from the subject. We are talking of farms, not diamonds."

"As to the farm, then, you are likely to be the only bidder, unless you allow the mortgage to remain."

"If I were inclined to do that I would not disturb you as long as you paid the interest promptly."

"Then you decline to buy the farm at private sale?"

"I do."

"I don't think you will be any better off in the end, Squire Hudson, for oppressing a poor man and robbing him of his little all," said Mark Nelson, bitterly.

"You don't look at the matter from a business point of view," said the squire, coldly. "I am acting as any business man would under the circumstances."

"I cannot believe you, sir. All business men are not so hard-hearted."

"I really don't think there is any use in prolonging this interview," said Squire Hudson, stiffly. "I have resolved upon my course, in which I am perfectly justified, however you may choose to regard it."

This removed the farmer's last hope, and he had only to look about for another home for his family. There was small choice of houses in the little farming town. In fact there was but one house--a shabby, dilapidated building, a mile from the church and store. This, Mr. Nelson, having no choice, engaged for a period of three months.

"It makes me homesick to think of going to live in that barn," said Sarah, as they were sitting together after supper.

"It may not be so bad as you think, Sarah," said her mother, but she secretly sympathized with her daughter.

"I wish Squire Hudson had to live there himself," said Walter, in an angry outburst.

Usually Walter was checked by his father when uttering such speeches, but tonight Mark Nelson took no notice of his son's angry remark. He felt that it would only be a righteous retribution upon the squire for his cold selfishness.

While they were sitting in the plain room endeared to them by the association of years, a sound of wheels was heard, and the village stage stopped before the door.

"Who can it be?" said Sarah, wonderingly.

The whole family hurried to the window. What youthful, yet manly figure, was that actively descending from his perch beside the driver?

"It's Tom!" exclaimed Mrs. Nelson. "Heaven be praised! It is my dear boy."

Tom was almost suffocated by the embraces which he received on entering the house.

"How you have grown, Tom!" said Sarah. "And how well you look!"

"Thank you for the compliment," said Tom, laughing. "But I don't feel well."

"What is the matter?" asked his mother, with maternal solicitude.

"I am as hungry as a bear. Have you got anything to eat in the house?"

This hint was enough. Fresh tea was made, and the wanderer was soon sitting before a bountiful supply of food, cooked in his mother's best style.

"It seems good to be at home," said Tom, looking around him, his face beaming with happiness.

"Did you get my letter, Tom, announcing the squire's intention to foreclose the mortgage?" asked his father, gravely.

"Yes, father. Is it really true?"

"Yes, he will listen to no persuasions."

"When does the sale take place?"

"Tomorrow."

"I shall be present. Have you thought of any other house, father?"

"The old Belcher house is the only one I can hire."

"That is a poor place."

"It must do for lack of a better."

"I didn't think the squire would act so meanly. At any rate, father, I will see that you don't any of you suffer for lack of money."

"Have you been doing well, Tom?" asked Walter.

"Ask me tomorrow, Walter. Tonight I want to hear all the news, and everything that has happened since I went away."

CHAPTER XXXI

BIDDING FOR THE FARM

"I apprehend," said the squire to his brother-in-law the next morning, "that we shall get the farm at our own price."

"I hope we shall, squire," said the poor relative, deferentially. "I suppose this man Nelson is sorry to part with it."

"Of course. He charges me with meanness, oppressing the poor, and so on, but of course I don't mind that. It's a matter of business, as I told him."

"To be sure."

"I am not to be moved by sentimental considerations. Business is business, but he won't see it in that light."

"You consider the farm worth considerable more than the amount of the mortgage, of course?"

"It is worth four thousand dollars, in my opinion," said the squire, complacently.

"If you get it for twenty-two hundred, it will be an excellent bargain."

"Father," exclaimed Sinclair, entering the breakfast room, rather hurriedly, "Tom Nelson has got home."

"Where did you hear this, my son?" asked Squire Hudson, in surprise.

"At the store. He got home by coach last evening."

"Got discontented, I suppose," said the squire, in a tone of triumph. "I thought that was how it would turn out. He can't expect me to advance money to take him out there again."

"I wish you would let me go," said Sinclair.

"Some day I may take a trip out there with you, my son. Have you seen Thomas?"

"No, he keeps mighty close. He hasn't even been round at the store."

"He is ashamed to show himself, I suppose. He will have to work on the farm--on a farm again."

"I suppose that will be a hard pill for him to swallow," said Sinclair.

"No doubt. He is poor and proud, like his father before him. I am glad of one thing--that I am sure of getting back the two hundred dollars I advanced for his journey. I wonder where he raised money to get back."

*****

Though there were not likely to be any competitors for the farm, a considerable number gathered at the sale. There was a general feeling of sympathy for the Nelsons, but no one was able to express that sympathy in a tangible form. Squire Hudson cared little for the opinion of his neighbors. Some of them were in debt to him, and he looked down upon them with the arrogance of wealth.

Tom received many friendly greetings. He was plainly dressed, quiet in his manner and seemed to take matters very coolly.

At length the farm was put up, the auctioneer naturally turning towards the squire, who responded pompously, "I bid twenty-two hundred dollars, the amount of the mortgage I hold upon the property."

"Is there any other bid?" asked the auctioneer.

"I bid twenty-five hundred dollars," said a clear, boyish voice.

All were startled, and all eyes were turned upon Tom Nelson, who came slightly forward.

"Twenty-five hundred!" repeated the auctioneer, hesitating whether he should receive the bid.

"I protest against this outrage," exclaimed Squire Hudson, angrily. "The bid is ridiculous."

"Why is my bid ridiculous, Squire Hudson?" asked Tom, calmly.

"Because you haven't got the money. It is a transparent attempt to run up the price of the farm."

"You know nothing of my circumstances, Squire Hudson," said Tom, independently. "I stand ready to pay the sum I bid, and, should you outbid me, I am ready to prove to any committee you may appoint, that I possess the money, or all my bids shall go for nothing, and you can have the farm at your first offer."

"That is fair!" cried all.

"This is all nonsense," said the squire. "Those of you who choose may believe this boy, I don't."

"Going at twenty-five hundred!" said the auctioneer.

"Twenty-five hundred and fifty!" said the squire, adding, "I make the bid on the terms proposed by the boy."

137

"Twenty-eight hundred!" said Tom.

"And fifty!" bid the squire.

"Three thousand!" instantly came from Tom.

No one was more surprised than Tom's own family at this unexpected scene. He had not dropped a hint as to his intentions, choosing to take all by surprise. Mark Nelson was perplexed. Though he had great confidence in Tom, he feared that he could not make good his bold bids.

At length the farm was knocked down to our hero at three thousand five hundred dollars.

"Now," said the squire, angrily, "I demand that this farce come to an end. I believe the bidding of this boy to be a premeditated swindle. If so, I will do my best to have him punished."

"And I," said Tom, boldly, "have an equal right to demand that Squire Hudson submit proof that he is responsible for the amount of his offers."

"Curse your impudence!" exclaimed the squire, foaming with rage.

"But I waive that right," continued Tom, "and will ask Squire Hudson to name two gentlemen present to examine the proofs which I have to offer of my ability to back my bids."

"I name Mr. Jones and Mr. Howe," said the squire, quickly, "and request them to act at once."

"That is my desire," said Tom.

In five minutes the committee reported that Tom had shown them bank-books, of two Boston banks, certifying that he held two thousand dollars on deposit in one, and four thousand in the other.

"Is that satisfactory?" asked Tom, coolly.

"No," shouted the squire, "I believe that the books are bogus."

But the rest of those present entertained no doubts, and our hero was at once surrounded by admiring friends, who shook his hand till it fairly ached.

"Squire Hudson, your mortgage shall be paid whenever you desire," said Tom.

"Three cheers for Tom Nelson!" proposed someone, and the cheers were given with a will. During the confusion the squire and his brother-in-law slipped out of the house, thoroughly discomfited.

CHAPTER XXXII

MANHOOD

If Squire Hudson was surprised at Tom's suddenly revealed wealth, Mr. Nelson was no less so. When Tom first commenced bidding, his father feared that he was only trying to annoy the squire or, perhaps, seeking to force him to pay a higher price for the farm. But when investigation revealed the fact of Tom's riches, and he saw the mountain of debt lifted from his little property, he was overjoyed and grateful.

"I can't understand it, Tom," he said, "how could you possibly get possession of so much money?"

"I have worked hard, father, but that won't explain it. I have been very lucky, and my good luck has enabled me to save the farm."

"I think you will be easier with me than the squire, Tom," said his father, smiling. "I will make out a mortgage to you, since your money has been used to redeem the farm."

"I shall have no claim on the farm," said Tom, "or if I have I give it to you. I have money enough for myself and hope to earn a good deal more besides."

"If that is the case, Tom, I will gladly accept your gift. It will be a great relief to think that I have no interest to pay. Now I shall be able to get along easily. I have over two hundred dollars on hand."

"I want to make your life easier, hereafter, father. I think you need a larger income than the farm will yield you, and I will therefore send you a hundred dollars every quarter."

"You are very generous, Tom, but I fear you will soon get rid of all your money at this rate."

"I will explain my circumstances, father, and then you will think differently. I have a business in San Francisco which will yield me at least a thousand dollars a year, without my personal attention, and after paying the squire what is due him I shall have about four thousand dollars left. This I mean to invest securely in Boston."

"I can hardly realize that you are so rich, Tom."

"I can scarcely realize it myself, father. When I think of the change that fifteen months have made in my circumstances I consider myself the luckiest boy in the world and have great cause for gratitude."

139

It will be understood that, though Tom had bid thirty-five hundred dollars for the farm, all he was required to pay was the amount of the mortgage, the bid having been made in his father's interest. In a few days the business was completed, and Mr. Nelson found himself the owner of an unencumbered property.

Tom remained a week longer in the village and then started once more for California. His mother urged him to remain at home, now that he had so much money, but Tom reminded her that he was partner in a business in San Francisco and that he needed to look after his interests there. John Miles might be sick, or die, and in that case he might meet with serious losses.

Returning to San Francisco Tom became an active instead of a silent partner. The business was considerably enlarged and became much more profitable. At the end of two years Tom sold out to his partner for several thousand dollars, and, entering an office, studied law, devoting a portion of his time to general study. At a comparatively early age he was admitted to the bar of his adopted city and, by degrees, got into lucrative practice. He had become so much attached to California that he decided to make it his permanent home.

Up among the New Hampshire hills his father still tills his little farm, but he no longer depends upon it for his entire living. Tom regularly sends the allowance he promised, and in addition his brothers are often the recipients of handsome gifts. Harry, developing a taste for study, was sent to Exeter Academy, from which in due course he was transferred to Harvard. He, too, was destined for the law, and when he had taken his legal degree, he joined Tom in California and is now his partner.

Other changes there are in the little village. Squire Hudson is dead, and Sinclair, making haste to sell the homestead, moved to New York, engaged in speculation, and lost everything. One day, shabbily dressed, he entered Tom's office in San Francisco and asked for the loan of fifty dollars to enable him to reach the mines. Tom gave it, for old acquaintance' sake. It was not the last request for money made by Sinclair. Nothing has been heard of him for some years, and it is probable that a life which was of no service to any one is finished. He had the best start in life but misused his advantages. Tom has worthily employed the talents committed to his charge and is happy, honored, and prosperous.

THE END

TEACHERS GUIDE QUESTIONS FOR THE YOUNG MINER

1.   In Chapter I, Tom, Mr. Ferguson, Captain Fletcher and Mr. Peabody talk about how much they would like to earn from the mines. Tom says that he would be very satisfied with $5,000. How much is this today? How much does Mr. Peabody want to make? Does his work ethic match this goal? How do you predict Mr. Peabody will succeed?

2.   In Chapter IV, before John Miles departs for San Francisco, he and Mr. Ferguson compare instances of hard work to chances of mere luck. What examples does John Miles provide to prove his point, and what does Mr. Ferguson argue? Who do you agree with and why? Do you have a different opinion of luck?

3.   Chapter VII is titled "The Heathen Chinee." What does the way that Alger describes Chinese men tell you about how they were perceived during this time period? How has language and representation of groups of people changed over time? In this same chapter, Alger mentions Bret Harte twice. Who is Bret?

4.   John Miles and Bill Crane both happen upon the same lonely house in the woods. How does each man approach Mrs. Brown in his first moments of acquaintance? How does each man react to the marriage proposal? What does this tell you about each man's character? Give specific examples.

5.   Ebenezer Onthank makes several assumptions about Tom and Mr. Ferguson in Chapters XV and XVI relating first to nut-cakes, then their sleeping habits and finally about Tom's marksmanship. Describe these assumptions in detail, and what Mr. Onthank concludes. Was Mr. Onthank correct in making them?

6.   Describe Mark Nelson and Squire Hudson's meeting in Chapter XIX. Who do you believe is correct?

7.   At the end of Chapter XX, Mr. Ferguson takes less than his share of the profits he and Tom make from the sale of the wagon. What reason does Mr. Ferguson give to Tom for doing so? How has this reason motivated Tom throughout his journey and during his work?

8.   In Chapter XXII, Mr. Ferguson and Tom save Richard Russell's life. Name three ways Mr. Ferguson and Tom are rewarded for saving his life.

9.   At the auction for Mr. Nelson's farm, why does Squire Hudson disbelieve that Tom has enough money to counter his offer? What beliefs prevent him from accepting that Tom can pay for the mortgage?

10. After his family is able to stay on their farm, what does Tom do? What qualities does he have that you think will help him succeed? Name three and explain why you chose those three.

TEACHERS GUIDE ANSWERS FOR THE YOUNG MINER

1. Five thousand dollars in 1849 is worth roughly $151,500 today. Mr. Peabody would like to earn $50,000, but his work ethic does not match his goal. He expects gold very easy to come by.

2. John Miles argues that when "when two men work side by side with equal industry and one finds a nugget worth thousands of dollars while the other plods along at a few dollars a day," there is some luck in the former finding a large nugget of gold. He also argues that it is luck when one man is born to a wealthy family and one born to a poor family and hard work.

3. Mr. Ferguson does not so readily attribute success to luck. He argues that, "what we call good luck, generally comes from greater industry, good judgment, and, above all, the prompt use of opportunities." When Miles gives the example of a man born to wealth and a man born to poverty, Ferguson purports that in this case the one born to poverty is luckier because he is removed from temptation. Thus he believes in some types of luck, but holds true that hard work is what brings success.

4. Alger portrays Chinese men as sly, cunning and heathen, and this was how many people perceived them. Language and representation of language has changed over time because today we are more conscious to not group people together and draw broad conclusions about them. We also try to avoid generalizations that are negative. Bret Harte was an American author and poet who depicted and described the American West and pioneering life in California in the mid- to late 1800s.

5. John Miles is polite to Mrs. Brown and honestly confesses that he has no money to give her in exchange for food. He concludes that she is a strong, determined woman who can fend for herself, and when she proposes marriage to him, Miles gracefully declines. Bill Crane, on the other hand, tries to avoid paying for a meal though Mrs. Brown later offers it for free. He becomes so excited at the thought of her fortune that he agrees to marry her even though he knows little about her. These two encounters further reveal that John Miles is a level-headed, honest and thoughtful man and that Bill Crane is a bit sneaky, overly concerned with money reactionary.

6.   Ebenezer Onthank is astonished that Mr. Ferguson is not familiar with nut-cakes, and he implies that Mr. Ferguson is peculiar. Only after his shock do they realize that nut-cakes go by a different name where Mr. Ferguson comes from. When Tom and Mr. Ferguson sleep later than Onthank, he assumes that the former two are naturally lazy, though the reader understands this not to be the case. Lastly, Onthank urges Tom to give him the gun because he believes Tom to be too young and inexperienced to have accurate aim. In all three assumptions, Onthank is incorrect.

7.   During Mark Nelson and Squire Hudson's meeting, the squire continuously points to the business aspects of the loan. He has no sympathy for Mark Nelson's pleas for understanding – the squire refuses to take the drought, or the fact that they are neighbors and should be friendly, into consideration.

8.   Mr. Ferguson explains that he never could have bought the wagon if Tom did not contribute his share. Ferguson also says he is glad to help a boy who is helping and working for his family. The thought of his family and their financial needs motivates Tom to work hard and to succeed.

9.   Mr. Ferguson and Tom are rewarded for saving Richard Russell's life by making a new friend, by discovering a new, rich mining camp and by later selling the camp to new miners.

10.   Squire Hudson does not believe Tom has enough money to counter his offer because Tom is so young and he cannot fathom Tom having the sufficient funds. The squire assumes it is a blatant trick to raise the bidding price and make the squire pay more. After his family is able to stay on their farm, Tom returns to California to attend to his business. He works on it for several years before selling his share, studying law and becoming an attorney.

VOCABULARY WORDS FOR
THE YOUNG MINER

bonanza: a situation or event that creates a sudden increase in wealth, good fortune, or profits

"'Tom,' he exclaimed, in excitement, 'do you see that, and that? I believe you've struck a bonanza.'"

cupidity: a greed for money or possessions

Miles confessed to himself with sadness that he had been imprudent to leave the bag where it would naturally excite the cupidity of any passing adventurer.

deign: to do something that one considers to be beneath one's dignity

Bruin deigned no reply, but continued to survey him with steady, unwinking eyes.

epicure: a person who takes considerable pleasure in fine food and drink

It might not have attracted an epicure, but neither of the three was fastidious...

espied: to catch sight of

Presently he espied the two Chinamen.

expostulate: to express strong disapproval or disagreement

"Now, Tom Scott," expostulated the landlord, "this ain't fair. I want the wagon more'n you do, and you're a-raisin' the price on me."

goluptious: splendid, delightful or magnificent

"If you ever come to Green Mountain Mills, I'll get marm to fry a batch of nut-cakes, and you'll say they're goluptious."

guileless: free of deceit; artless

But, guileless as they seemed, they had proved more than a match for Bill Crane and his victim.

lugubrious: looking or sounding sad or dismal

Crane stared at the deceptive bag in the most lugubrious astonishment.

ocular: relating to the eyes or vision

Bill Crane took another look at the contents of the bag, hoping that he had been deceived by some ocular delusion, but the second examination brought him no comfort.

pecuniary: of, relating to, or consisting of money.

Again, he had reason to think that the arrangement would benefit Tom and himself in a pecuniary way, and the Scotchman was by no means indifferent to that consideration, though, as we have seen, he did not unduly exalt the power or value of money.

prudential: involving or showing care and forethought, typically in business

Bill Crane had not filled the bag with sand and thrown it away from prudential considerations,

sward: an expanse of short grass

He selected as his breakfast table the green sward beside a sparkling mountain streamlet.

vaquero: (in Spanish-speaking parts of the US) a cowboy or a cattle driver

A shout caused Tom suddenly to turn his head, and to his joy he saw a mounted Mexican vaquero, who had brought him timely relief.

victual: food or provisions as prepared for consumption

"If you'll wait long enough for me to make some hot tea and warm the victuals, you shall have a chance to judge of my cookin'."

wanton: (of a cruel or violent action) deliberate and unprovoked

Miles decided that for some unknown reason the thief had transferred its contents to some other bag--perhaps his own--and then had discarded the original one, in wanton humor filling it instead with sand.

COMMENTARY FOR
THE YOUNG ADVENTURER AND
THE YOUNG MINER

by Rick Newcombe

While the early Horatio Alger stories took place in New York City, some of the later stories were set on the West Coast or they focused on traveling from New York to San Francisco in the 1870s. The Young Adventurer is mainly about the journey, while The Young Miner shows us what happens after they arrive.

Thomas Nelson is the hero of both books. We follow his exploits as he travels more than 3,000 miles by train, steamboat and horseback, all when he is barely 16 years old. This was an era before planes and automobiles had even been invented.

Tom's "Stories of Success" are absolutely amazing, and they are pure Horatio Alger.

We first meet Tom when he is with his father, mother, brothers and sisters on their dirt-poor farm in New Hampshire. We learn that the richest man in town, Squire Hudson, is cruel and heartless, while Tom's struggling father, Mark Nelson, is warm and loving. These are not unusual characterizations -- of nasty rich people and kind poor people -- in Horatio Alger stories.

Despite the widespread misconception that Horatio Alger was an advocate for the rich, Alger's view of money was far more nuanced. Wealth can be great, he said, and it can be awful. It can be used for good: to feed the hungry, for instance; and it can be used for evil: to force a family out of their home.

Mark Nelson's heart is filled with love and happiness, particularly since his wife, who was known as Mary Dale when they met, is so beautiful and cheerful. We learn that Squire Hudson still harbors a grudge because he wanted to marry her, but she said no and chose Mark Nelson instead. Hudson secretly vows to get even by plotting to drive the Nelsons off their farm and into the poorhouse. "When she and her children are paupers, she may regret the slight she put upon me," he says to himself.

Alger's writing style is witty, his plots are ingenious and his dialogue is clear, easy to understand and, at times, brilliant. For instance, when he wants to tell the reader that Squire Hudson's wife is not beautiful compared with Mary Nelson, he does so by allowing us to hear the squire's thoughts. His wife is talking about Mrs. Nelson, and says she is with Mark Nelson only because she did not have any other proposals of marriage, not knowing that her own husband had proposed to Mary.

The squire replied:

"'Probably she did (have other proposals), for she was a very pretty girl.'

"'Then she's faded,' said Mrs. Hudson, tossing her head.

"Squire Hudson did not reply; but as his eyes rested on the sharp, querulous face of his helpmate, and he compared it mentally with the pleasant face of Mrs. Nelson, he said to himself that, faded or not, the latter was still better looking than his wife had been in the days of her youth. Of course it would not do to say so, for Mrs. Hudson was not amiable."

Tom senses danger for his family during their discussion about finances, and he wants to do something about it. His sister and father comment about the unequal distribution of wealth. It doesn't seem fair that one family would have so much and another so little. But Horatio Alger was no socialist, and Americans in the 1870s looked to their own initiative -- not government handouts -- for creating wealth.

Publisher's Weekly magazine asserts that Horatio Alger helped form the American character, and in the 21st century, we still strive for material success through hard work, rather than taking it from others. As the columnist Charles Krauthammer said, "Americans, generally speaking, don't envy the rich. They want to be rich."

There was little chance for Tom to get rich or help his family financially if he stayed on the New Hampshire farm. It appears that the family had already moved once, from New Jersey. But this time Tom knew he would have to travel west to find his fortune. The California gold rush was in the newspapers, and Tom set a goal to join the thousands of other prospectors.

He had no money to buy tickets for traveling such a long distance. How could he possibly even begin? Horatio Alger tells us:

"The world was all before him where to choose. His available capital was small, it is true, amounting only to thirty-seven cents and a jack-knife; but he had, besides, a stout heart, a pair of strong hands, an honest face, and plenty of perseverance -- not bad equipment for a young adventurer."

This was Horatio Alger's way of telling us that the intangible virtues of courage, strength, honesty and perseverance are more important than money. If you live your life with these virtues, the money will follow.

The issue of honesty comes up repeatedly in both books, which is not surprising, considering that most Americans view honesty as one of the most important character traits of successful people. For instance, we have all heard the stories about George Washington admitting to chopping down a cherry tree, saying, "I cannot tell a lie," and Abraham Lincoln walking a long distance to return some change after a store clerk had given him too much. True or not, they are part of this nation's mythology.

Tom Nelson's honesty does not always pay off immediately -- in fact, at one point it looks like he might be put in jail -- but in the end, honesty does prove to be the best policy.

Tom has remarkable courage. He takes calculated risks in a series of thrilling adventures in both books, and he succeeds over and over.

Throughout the stories, Horatio Alger creates characters with opposing character traits, which helps the reader see the contrast between right and wrong. For instance, we see Sinclair Hudson, the arrogant son of the squire, who is lazy and envious while Tom is industrious and generous. We see the swindlers and thieves, Milton Graham and his friend Vincent, and Bill Crane in another episode, all of whom keep tripping over themselves and failing in their devious designs.

We see other thieves in The Young Miner, including two Chinese men, who are referred to as "heathens" and "Chinamen," which was typical of the times. Mark Twain wrote a newspaper story defending Chinese workers in Northern California, and he referred to them as "Chinamen," which I'm sure he meant as a term of endearment. Today, that word is considered offensive, but in the 1870s, it was not.

Native Americans don't fare much better. Native Americans were called "savages" and worse in the writings of the time, so it is not surprising to see similar descriptions in Horatio Alger stories.

The last Horatio Alger novel was written years before the passage of Prohibition, and we have no idea what Alger's political views on the subject were, but it is clear that the author was anti-alcohol in his own life. He creates a realistic fight scene in a saloon involving a temperance man from Scotland, Donald Ferguson, and a fall-down drunk American who is totally obnoxious in the Missouri tavern. Alger also was resolutely opposed to tobacco, though an occasional praiseworthy character can be seen enjoying a pipe after dinner. It was mainly the boys and young men who spent their money on cigars while visiting pool halls and saloons that he mocked.

Wearing nice clothes was so important during this time period. If you were poor, you wore rags. If you had some money, you could afford nice clothes. As part of that emphasis on appearance, a pocket watch, or vest watch, was considered a status symbol. When Tom acquires one as a gift, he agrees with his donor, Mr. Waterbury, that on the first day he will check the time every few minutes, just as Mr. Waterbury did when he was a young man with his first watch.

Let me offer two unrelated comments about the vest watch because I believe it carries great significance. First, it is important that Tom had asked his mother to sew in an extra pocket for this watch, although at the time he had neither a watch nor even the slightest prospect of obtaining one. Still, he had faith and optimism. He expected that someday he would indeed have such a watch. By having his mother sew the pocket in his vest, he was using what we today call "visualization" to achieve his goal.

Paul J. Meyer, founder of the company Success Motivation Institute, recorded a powerful speech called "The Power of Goal Setting," in which he talked about the importance of expecting positive results. He cited Charles Kettering's "birdcage theory." Kettering headed up the research department at General Motors for 20 years and was responsible for the electrical starting motor and leaded gasoline. He said that if you were to buy a birdcage and put it in your room, it would be only a matter of time before you succumbed and put a bird in it. Along the same lines, Tom Nelson had asked his mother to sew in a pocket for his vest watch, which created a constant reminder, a forced visualization, of what he wanted, and it was only a matter of time before he got the watch.

Horatio Alger was a century and a half ahead of today's motivational writers, who say the same thing but probably are unaware that they are standing on his shoulders. If you want a contemporary example, look at this passage from Rhonda Byrne's bestselling book, The Secret, which was first published in 2006. She tells the story of a woman who found her "perfect partner" by doing precisely what Tom Nelson's mother did for him by sewing that pocket:

"Then one day as she arrived home and was parking her car in the middle of her garage, she gasped as she realized that her actions were contradicting what she wanted. If her car was in the middle of the garage, there was no room for her perfect partner's car! Her actions were powerfully saying to the Universe that she did not believe she was going to receive what she had asked for. So she immediately cleaned up her garage and parked her car to one side, leaving space for her perfect partner's car on the other side."

The second observation involves the issue of how so many things of the past come back in a different form in the present. Isn't it interesting how, for more than a century after the Horatio Alger stories were first printed, most people checked the time by wearing wristwatches? They would not reach into their pockets to find a timepiece. Yet, in the 21st century, if you ask someone the time, more often than not they will reach into their pockets to check the time on their smart phone.

This is one of the most fascinating aspects of reading Horatio Alger stories -- to see America as it was between 1865 and 1900. This was a time when nearly everyone was consumed with getting rich. Mark Twain called it the "Gilded Age." Reading the Horatio Alger Series gives many details of America at the time, both externally -- the hardships, the crudeness of life without running water or electricity -- and internally, which includes the way they thought. This has been called the "climate of opinion." Money was a constant topic of conversation, and government was hardly mentioned at all. For many years after the Civil War, the federal government in Washington, D.C., was not an important part of the lives of most Americans.

At the end of The Young Miner, we see that Tom is indeed on the path to great riches. He has been able to help his family out, and he is totally independent, becoming a wealthy merchant in San Francisco. (If you want to know the value of his wealth in today's dollars, Google the words "inflation calculator," and you will find a number of websites that will help you calculate the answer.)

He also shows a generous spirit by giving the hapless Sinclair Hudson money as a favor because he is so downtrodden.

Tom Nelson lives his life with an air of "positive expectancy." He is always cheerful and optimistic. He is poised and confident. For instance, when a servant tells him to go to the back door, he politely stands his ground. He embraces hard work. He is courageous when encountering new adventures, even when it looks like the American Indians might kill him.

In other words, he is the original embodiment of the values embraced in what has become, over the years, a multibillion-dollar self-improvement industry. Horatio Alger spelled out the keys to success and happiness, not with a list of rules or principles, but by creating the ideal boy as he becomes a man. He called his central characters "heroes" because they represent the ultimate personification of the ideal young man, as he grows from adolescence, on his exciting and prosperous adventures in these inspiring "Stories of Success."

Rick Newcombe is the founder and CEO of Creators Syndicate, Creators Publishing and Sumner Books.

THE LIFE AND THEMES OF
HORATIO ALGER, JR.

By Stefan Kanfer

The Merriam-Webster Dictionary devotes one sentence to him: "Of, relating to, or resembling the fiction of Horatio Alger in which success is achieved through self-reliance and hard work."

True as far as it goes, but that sentence reveals nothing about the man or his accomplishment. Then again, other contemporary reference books are just as terse. Not one acknowledges that Alger in his day (circa 1880-1920) was a publishing phenomenon. During those decades, when a sale of 10,000 volumes was deemed a triumph, readers bought more than 200 million copies of Alger's works, placing him in a league with J.K. Rowling and Stephen King.

Alas, today most of his novels—and there are more than 100—are out of print. But not for long. Thanks to the resuscitation efforts of Sumner Books, a division of Creators Syndicate, Alger's best literary productions are being furnished with fresh covers, new fonts and energetic promotion.

Seldom has there been a more relevant illustration of the maxim that what goes around comes around. At the turn of the 19th century, Alger was the standard-bearer of a phenomenally successful experiment in social reform and personal improvement. That movement inspired disadvantaged kids to move on up, leading juvenile delinquents into productive, significant lives. Men as different as Groucho Marx and Ernest Hemingway were fans.

"Horatio Alger's books conveyed a powerful message to me," wrote Marx, "and to many of my young friends as well—that if you worked hard at your trade, the big chance would eventually come. As a child I didn't regard it as a myth, and as an old man I think of it as the story of my life."

Hemingway's sister Marcelline recalled that during their childhood, "There was one summer when Ernest couldn't get enough of Horatio Alger." Not that Alger's boys' books influenced Papa's prose style. But there must have been something in the writer's stress on grit and self-reliance that affected young Ernest, as it did so many of his contemporaries.

By the end of the Roaring Twenties, though, Horatio Alger had become as passé as the Ford Model T. During the Depression he fared no better; Nathaniel West's satirical 1934 novel, A Cool Million, sent Alger's plots in reverse, as the naïve protagonist loses limb after limb seeking success among rapacious capitalists. Decades later, the film adaptation of Hunter Thompson's 1971 novel, Fear and Loathing in Las Vegas, presented the antihero as "Horatio Alger gone mad on drugs in Las Vegas."

What lay behind Alger's ability to enchant so many Americans—and to enrage so many others? The author's story furnishes a trove of clues:

The sickly child of a Unitarian minister in Marlborough, Massachusetts, Horatio, born in 1832, was always the smallest in his class and far from an academic star. Still, his report cards were good enough for admission to Harvard. There his academic prowess was in inverse proportion to his size (5 feet 2 inches). He won prizes, published verse and fiction in undergraduate magazines, and labeled the entire four years a period of "unmixed happiness."

Decades would pass before he found such contentment again. Upon graduation, Horatio attempted to make his way as a writer. After five unsuccessful years, he returned to Harvard, this time to study at the Divinity School. In 1860 the Reverend Horatio Alger was named minister of the First Parish Unitarian Church of Brewster on Cape Cod. Salary: $800 per year. To supplement his meager income, he turned once again to writing. This time, his stories were well-received, and he allowed himself to dream of a dual career of preacher and writer. That's when catastrophe struck.

It was of his own making, if one historian is to be believed. According to this claim, a 13-year-old told his parents that the new parson had made advances to him. An investigation began. Another lad made a similar complaint. Faced with charges of behaving inappropriately, the accused was allowed to resign—with the proviso that he leave town at once.

Sometime later, Horatio wrote a poem about one Friar Anselmo, who had committed an unspecified crime. Melancholy and remorseful, he comes across a wounded traveler and gives him aid. Whereupon an angel materializes and offers salvation:

Thy guilty stains shall be washed white again
By noble service done thy fellow man.

The fugitive repaired to New York City in the spring of 1866, resolved to live out the Christian ideal, expiating his sin by saving others. The Manhattan he entered was the epicenter of the Gilded Age, a magnet for millions of ambitious climbers, drawn by the post-Civil War boom. Out of sight of the glittering prosperity, the mansions and carriages, however, was another New York, a squalid night town that travelers compared to Calcutta, India.

In The Good Old Days, They Were Terrible, historian Otto Bettmann reports that there was scarcely a slum that pedestrians could negotiate "without climbing over a heap of trash or, in rain, wading through a bed of slime." Many streets were so dangerous that policemen hesitated to walk them alone. A Gramercy Park resident noted in his diary, "Most of my friends are investing in revolvers and carry them about at night"—and the Park was one of the city's better neighborhoods.

The New York City street urchin entered the national consciousness in those years. More than 60,000 neglected or abandoned kids ran unsupervised in the street, partly because of the fallout from the tidal waves of immigration from Europe and partly because of families broken by the Civil War.

What was to be done about these juveniles likely to die on the streets or to end up behind bars? The Reverend Charles Loring Brace founded the Children's Aid Society, designed to take homeless or abused kids away from their corrosive environments. At the same time, John Hughes, New York's first Roman Catholic archbishop, set up parochial schools and a residential institution called the Catholic Protectory, which brought up abandoned or orphaned children to be useful members of society.

Horatio Alger joined these efforts at reclamation. He, too, asked himself what could be done about homeless children. Seeking answers, he wandered through the city's worst neighborhoods. He interviewed "street arabs" who spoke of broken homes, violent confrontations with parents, doomed futures. He observed how their cocky attitudes masked a profound despair. He advised them to get real jobs instead of hanging about, squandering whatever came their way from shining shoes or picking pockets. A handful nodded in agreement, expressing the desire to change their lives; most were content to take life as they found it.

Why, he pondered, did individuals subjected to the same conditions turn out so differently? One boy might become a thief, a sociopath, even a killer. His neighbor, perhaps his brother, might aim to be an upright citizen. What was the difference between them?

What saved certain boys, he came to believe, was a quality that gave them the strength to resist sloth and temptation. In a word, character. But was this inborn? In that case determinism won the day, and change was out of the question. Or, given the right opportunity and attitude, could a dispossessed youth win his share of the American dream? The latter, Alger believed—but only if the boy stopped regarding himself as a victim.

As Alger meditated upon the worst crime of the slums—the stealing of childhood from children—an idea came to him. He would be Brother Anselmo redivivus. He had sinned against youths; now he would rescue them—and in the process save himself. As the novelist put it, by depicting the situation of city waifs, he would "excite a deeper and more widespread sympathy in the public mind, as well as exert a salutary influence upon the class of whom he is writing, by setting before them inspiring examples of what energy, ambition, and an honest purpose may achieve."

Ragged Dick became the template of the fiction to follow. Subtitled Street Life in New York with the Boot Blacks, it charted the rise of a 14-year-old boy from poverty to prosperity. Dick Hunter is an adolescent with all odds against him. He has no family, he smokes, drinks alcohol when he can afford it—not very often on the small change he gets from shining gentlemen's shoes—and sleeps on gratings in the winter.

Yet something separates him from his fellow waifs. He refuses to pick pockets like the others, won't mock his elders, and yearns to "grow up 'spectable.'" His bearing and his innate decency attract the attention of upright New Yorkers. One introduces him to his church; another presents Dick with a few dollars.

The earnest youth resolves to become literate to save his money and live a clean life. One day on a walk near South Ferry he sees a toddler fall in the water. Without hesitation, Dick jumps in and saves the drowning child. In gratitude, the father, an affluent businessman, offers the rescuer a job in his office. Gainfully employed, the onetime vagabond Dick Hunter becomes Richard Hunter Esq., and shuts the door forever on the "old vagabond life which he hoped never to resume."

Naïve? Simplistic? To the jaded, the cynical and the ignorant, yes. But not to thousands of children trapped in the real world of poverty and early death. They got the message of Ragged Dick and demanded more Horatio Alger novels with more moral lessons for them to absorb. Those books changed—and in many cases saved—lives a century before Dr. Martin Luther King Jr. stated his belief that what mattered was not the color of one's skin but the content of one's character.

Today, if you listen closely you can hear, amid the jeers, the escalating sound of the last laugh. In 1947, the Horatio Alger Association was founded. It attracts more prominent men and women now than it did then. The group is dedicated to recognizing American leaders who rose, like Alger's young heroes, from humble origins "through honesty, hard work, self-reliance and perseverance." With grants to U.S. high-school students who have "faced and overcome great obstacles in their young lives," the association encourages them to emulate such enterprising and disparate members as Oprah Winfrey and Ray Kroc, Tom Brokaw and Maya Angelou, Stan Musial and Colin Powell.

They can all testify to the truths that lie between the covers of this volume. Turn the first few pages, and you'll understand why so many followed Horatio Alger's breathless, cliff-hanging chapters leading the way from skid row to success. And why so many more are about to read that map in a world where everything has changed—except the basic truths of life.

Stefan Kanfer is an award-winning writer for City Journal and the author of numerous best-selling books.

ABOUT HORATIO ALGER, JR.

Horatio Alger was born in 1832 in Chelsea, Massachusetts. He spent his early years in the small town and under the guidance of the church and his father, the town pastor, before the family moved just west of Boston to the town of Marlborough.

As a shy young boy, Alger poured himself into books and soon became a distinguished student. He studied at Harvard and Harvard Divinity School before becoming a minister. He practiced ministry for a few years near Boston and on Cape Cod, but he was distracted by his true passion: writing.

He loved to write, and by 1865 Alger had written a handful of stories, including Frank's Campaign and Paul Prescott's Charge. The latter was the first in a series of stories that would eventually lead to his great success. In 1866, Alger moved to New York to write poetry, newspaper stories and magazine articles. However, he was shocked to find so many homeless and forgotten children among the streets, an unfortunate consequence of the Civil War. He made it his duty to aid the condition of these lost children, both through his stories and by his continuous acts of benevolence.

Horatio Alger became a household name shortly after the Civil War when he began publishing stories in the form of serializations. These serializations were featured in magazines such as Student and Schoolmate and were later compiled as books. Alger's books became enormously popular, especially among teenage boys across the country, and they soon reached millions and millions of readers. Alger continued to produce several stories a year, and, in later years, wrote novels in and of themselves instead of novels from magazine serials.

The years immediately following the Civil War were the same years when the United States emerged as one nation on the road to becoming a worldwide empire. The years between 1865 and 1900 were the years of the empire builders, with the rags-to-riches stories of John D. Rockefeller, Andrew Carnegie, Cornelius Vanderbilt and Thomas Edison. They were the years that laid the foundation for Henry Ford and other business titans and for the spectacular growth of the American economy throughout the 20th century and through today. During these years, Alger published well over 100 stories, poems and novels that spoke to the timeless themes and successes of this era.

The theme of Alger's books is consistent: If you work hard, go the extra mile, are faithful and honest, show kindness and generosity, and maintain a cheerful, positive and optimistic attitude, you will succeed in creating financial security and happiness. On the other hand, if you lie, cheat, steal, are lazy or envious, and try to take advantage of other people, you will be doomed to failure and misery. Despite his background as a preacher, Alger does not make these points in a self-righteous or pontificating way. What he does instead -- just like the parables that Jesus told -- is to create stories that illustrate the virtues that lead to success. And the stories that Alger creates are no ordinary stories. Each one is filled with lively plots and twists and turns, ones that are always unexpected and keep the reader wanting to know what's going to happen next.

As Alger grew older, he continuously strived to write the Great American Novel, little realizing that the rags-to-riches stories he created were more influential than any other novelists'. He travelled out west in early 1877 searching for new material and returned near the end of the year, producing similar stories with a new western backdrop. By 1897, Alger was suffering from asthma, bronchitis and slight short-term memory loss. He moved in with his sister in South Natick, Massachusetts where he spent the last two years of his life.

Most people have never heard of Horatio Alger while some are vaguely familiar with the term "rags-to-riches." In the Alger family, it was the norm to burn correspondence and manuscripts, and this, coupled with Alger's shyness, has greatly kept him from history's limelight. Though too often forgotten today, Alger's works and the themes within them still affect the American psyche. Many assert that there is a lagging spirit in present American culture, that these inspiring stories are irrelevant. Young people are bombarded with external stimuli that make it difficult for them to get to know themselves. Wide-eyed innocence and childlike enthusiasm, once revered as admirable qualities, are sources of mockery and disdain, which makes cynicism and pessimism inevitable. Video games, television shows, movies and music are all aimed at titillating and at seeing who can be the most gritty, violent or shocking. More than a few commentators have used the word "degrading" to describe the assault that children encounter today.

This is unfortunate. Young people need heroes and role models today just as much as they did in the 1870s and '80s, when Alger was creating them at a feverish pace from his New York City apartment, writing as many as four books at a time. Publisher A.K. Loring asserted that Alger's books "captured the spirits of reborn America" for "above all you can hear the cry of triumph of the oppressed over the oppressor ... What Alger has done is to portray the soul – the ambitious soul – of the country." Years later, biographer Edwin P. Hoyt concludes that Alger is "a writer whose influence on the American scene has been so profound that it is hard to measure." Indeed, Alger's works made an overwhelming impression on American culture and society that are still alive with us today. It is for this reason that these classics must be brought to a new generation of readers.

OUR COMMITMENT TO
HORATIO ALGER

By Rick Newcombe

Sumner Books is totally committed to reviving interest in Horatio Alger, one of the best-selling authors of all time yet someone who has been all but forgotten today. I'd like to tell you how this project came about.

Probably the best starting point is to tell you a little about myself. I grew up in suburban Chicago, and my parents were religious and fundamentally optimistic in their outlook on life. They encouraged all eight of their children to be positive in our thinking and hope and pray for the best in all situations. In my adolescence, I discovered many of the self-help authors from the 20th century, including Dale Carnegie, Napoleon Hill and Norman Vincent Peale. I remember reading a small magazine in the 1970s, when I was in my 20s, called Success Unlimited and being inspired each month to work hard and stay positive. The publisher of this magazine was W. Clement Stone, who started his career selling insurance policies door to door and who went on to build Combined Insurance, which became part of Aon, one of the largest insurance companies in the world.

By the time Mr. Stone died in 2002, he was a very successful businessman, an extremely generous philanthropist and totally committed to spreading the gospel of positive thinking. I remember reading one of his books, The Success System That Never Fails, which was both an autobiography and a blueprint for achieving success. Stone told the story of spending a summer on a farm in Michigan when he was 12, getting fresh air, helping on the farm and enjoying picnics, carnivals and camping out.

W. Clement Stone

"But I'll never forget the first day I went upstairs to the attic," he wrote, "for there I met Horatio Alger. At least 50 of his books, dusty and weather-worn, were piled in the corner. I took one down to the hammock in the front yard and started to read."

Stone said he was so enthralled he couldn't stop. "I read through all of them that summer," he wrote.

He said the principle in each book was that "the hero became a success because he was a man of character -- the villain a failure because he deceived and embezzled. How many Alger books were sold? No one knows. Estimates range from 100 million to 300 million. We do know that his books inspired thousands of American boys from poor families to strive to do the right thing because it was right and to acquire wealth."

That was the first time I had heard of Horatio Alger, but it never occurred to me to try to find his books. Over the years, I founded Creators Syndicate, which became one of the most successful newspaper syndication companies in the world. I attribute much of our success to our positive thinking and upbeat attitude. We became a multimillion-dollar international corporation by syndicating a wide variety of journalists, celebrities and award-winning cartoonists.

As we were expanding into new businesses, e-books and audiobooks were a natural starting point because we work with so many talented writers and artists. But we also wanted to try new things. With that in mind, I remembered Mr. Stone's enthusiastic recommendation of Horatio Alger's books, and I decided to read some. Many were available as e-books, and I thoroughly enjoyed them.an

I had a good feeling whenever I was transported back to New York City as it was in 1870, when trains were called "cars" and there were no automobiles. There was a constant risk of crossing the streets without streetlights or walk signs. A number of years later, the Brooklyn Dodgers, now the Los Angeles Dodgers, got their name from the treacherous dodging of horses, wagons and streetcars that was required to cross the street in the city. In those days, plumbing with hot and cold running water was not taken for granted, much less radios, televisions, computers or smartphones. Are you kidding? A smartphone in the 1860s? There wasn't even a telephone.

But what great stories Alger wrote -- one after another. I couldn't get enough of them! And it was impossible not to feel grateful for all the modern conveniences of the 21st century when immersing myself in the world of America as it was in the 1860s and '70s.

As I read book after book, I felt like a teenager all over again, excited about the future and the promise of a brighter tomorrow. It was then that I decided to go full bore into spreading the word of Horatio Alger.

One of the problems with the e-books was the lack of organization; another was the maddening number of typos, over and over and over, or the lack of illustrations or the lack of a table of contents. In fact, what was intended to be a good deed to spread Mr. Alger's message really turned out to be something of a disservice.

So I made it my mission to have professional editors edit the texts so there were no typographical or spelling errors. We found appropriate illustrations. We included detailed tables of contents for each book, and we decided to publish them in groups, when appropriate, which has never been done before. We are including commentaries and teachers guides with each e-book.

We also decided to make audiobooks of as many of these "Stories of Success" as possible. We hired a terrific actor, Ben Gillman, and his initial experience shows you how far we have to go to spread the word. Ben went to the Hollywood public library to find some Horatio Alger books, but there was none. "You'd have to go to the downtown public library, in the historical section, to find those," the librarian told him.

Remember, this is one of the best-selling American authors of all time, yet it is as if he never existed.

Part of the problem is that some of the caricatures of Horatio Alger over the years have been absolutely brutal. Even to this day, the Encyclopedia Britannica, from which we expect objective reporting, calls Alger's dialogue and plots "outrageously bad." Come again? The encyclopedia is supposed to provide broad knowledge on specific subjects, not offer the biased literary criticism of a handful of editors. Talk about being unfair -- and just plain wrong!

How do you answer a cheap shot like that? Really, it is nothing more than an incredibly snooty opinion; in fact, it is an "outrageously bad" opinion. Remember, the Horatio Alger books were intended to be not great literature but rather inspirational stories to motivate young boys to achieve a better life. If the dialogue and plots were not lively and believable, the books would not have sold in the millions. The fact that Horatio Alger helped form the American character shows that an incredible number of boys ate up his books as thrilling and believable.

The brilliant writer Stefan Kanfer wrote an extensive review of Horatio Alger's works in 2000 for City Journal magazine, a publication of the prestigious Manhattan Institute. He started off believing the critics, but when he actually read some of Horatio Alger's books, he drew a totally different conclusion. "I began reading the novels aloud to my children," he wrote. "We found them well-plotted, entertaining, and instructive, not at all the righteous antiquities that I had been led to believe. Almost every chapter ends with a cliff-hanger, and all of us could hardly wait for the next night to find out what happened. The conclusions never failed to produce an emotional satisfaction and a feeling that what the author was selling -- independence, forbearance, square dealing -- was well worth buying."

We can only speculate about why the critics have been so harsh on Horatio Alger, but no doubt some it stems from their being turned off by precisely the character traits that Mr. Kanfer identifies. Like it or not, there is a mindset that scoffs at individual achievement through hard work, a positive attitude and generosity -- living every day with an "attitude of gratitude," which is the essence of Horatio Alger's message.

W. Clement Stone was routinely mocked for starting the day by saying, "I feel healthy! I feel happy! I feel terrific!" He encouraged his employees to do the same. In fact, he encouraged everyone to demonstrate outward enthusiasm and PMA, which stood for a positive mental attitude. His critics thought he was ridiculous, but Mr. Stone got the last laugh, living to age 100, which he had set as his goal, and accumulating hundreds of millions of dollars.

Roswell Crawford is an important character in Ragged Dick and Fame and Fortune because he oozes the world-owes-me-a-living attitude that is so common today. "Roswell was troubled with a large share of pride," Alger writes, "though it might have troubled himself to explain what he had to be proud of."

Roswell never understands the importance of integrity and its relationship to earning one's living. In fact, he once says that he would be happy to be paid $10 a week for nothing. "Well, if I get it, I don't care if I don't earn it," he says. In fact, Roswell is ashamed to be seen in the streets carrying a large bundle as part of a delivery for his job. Before being fired, his boss tells him, "You appear to think yourself of too great consequence to discharge properly the duties of your position."

Contrast that with Richard Hunter's attitude toward his entry-level job when he first starts working at the firm. "I'm ready to do anything that is required of me. I want to make myself useful," he says.

I have the impression that was the same attitude that Horatio Alger had as he approached his goal of becoming a successful writer who could change the world -- or at least the world of the thousands of homeless street urchins in the big city. It is difficult to imagine how bad their plight was. For instance, in 1874, which was seven years after Ragged Dick was first published, there was a little girl named Mary Ellen Wilson, who was beaten unmercifully by her stepmother. She was sent out into the streets ill-clothed in winter. There were other abuses, and they were horrible.

So a social worker named Etta Angel Wheeler wanted to intervene, to help get the child out of that environment. But there were no laws to protect children in such situations. Etta was desperate -- and clever. She enlisted the help of the American Society for the Prevention of Cruelty to Animals because animals were protected by law. Her attorneys argued that Mary Ellen, "as a member of the animal kingdom, deserved the same protection as abused animals." This led to new legislation and various child protective services.

Horatio Alger was at the forefront of this movement. He wanted to help the poor kids in the inner city, and he wound up not only helping them but inspiring millions of other young readers across the country. Many of them transformed their lives as a direct result of the inspiration of the "Stories of Success" that Horatio Alger managed to tell in one exciting setting after another.

It is not surprising that Ernest Hemingway's sister said that her brother could not get enough of Horatio Alger or that Walter Brennan, a famous actor for much of the 20th century, devoured his books. As the legendary Groucho Marx said: "Horatio Alger's books conveyed a powerful message to me and to many of my young friends -- that if you worked hard at your trade, the big chance would eventually come. As a child, I didn't regard it as a myth, and as an old man, I think of it as the story of my life."

Groucho was speaking for millions of Americans in the past and, we hope, millions more in the future.

Rick Newcombe is the founder and CEO of Creators Syndicate, Creators Publishing and Sumner Books.

PREVIEW OF ANOTHER ADVENTURE IN THE HORATIO ALGER "STORIES OF SUCCESS" SERIES

BOUND TO RISE

By Horatio Alger, Jr.

"Sit up to the table, children, breakfast's ready."

The speaker was a woman of middle age, not good-looking in the ordinary acceptation of the term, but nevertheless she looked good. She was dressed with extreme plainness, in a cheap calico; but though cheap, the dress was neat. The children she addressed were six in number, varying in age from twelve to four. The oldest, Harry, the hero of the present story, was a broad-shouldered, sturdy boy, with a frank, open face, resolute, though good-natured.

"Father isn't here," said Fanny, the second child.

"He'll be in directly. He went to the store, and he may stop as he comes back to milk."

The table was set in the center of the room, covered with a coarse tablecloth. The breakfast provided was hardly of a kind to tempt an epicure. There was a loaf of bread cut into slices, and a dish of boiled potatoes. There was no butter and no meat, for the family was very poor.

The children sat up to the table and began to eat. They were blessed with good appetites, and did not grumble, as the majority of my readers would have done, at the scanty fare. They had not been accustomed to anything better, and their appetites were not pampered by indulgence.

They had scarcely commenced the meal when the father entered. Like his wife, he was coarsely dressed. In personal appearance he resembled his oldest boy. His wife looking up as he entered perceived that he looked troubled.

Boiled potatoes: the modest meal we see the Walton family eating at the beginning of the story.

"What is the matter, Hiram?" she asked. "You look as if something had happened."

"Nothing has happened yet," he answered; "but I am afraid we are going to lose the cow."

"Going to lose the cow!" repeated Mrs. Walton in dismay.

168

"She is sick. I don't know what's the matter with her."

"Perhaps it is only a trifle. She may get over it during the day."

"She may, but I'm afraid she won't. Farmer Henderson's cow was taken just that way last fall, and he couldn't save her."

"What are you going to do?"

"I have been to Elihu Perkins, and he's coming over to see what he can do for her. He can save her if anybody can."

The children listened to this conversation, and, young as they were, the elder ones understood the calamity involved in the possible loss of the cow. They had but one, and that was relied upon to furnish milk for the family, and, besides a small amount of butter and cheese, not for home consumption, but for sale at the store in exchange for necessary groceries. The Waltons were too poor to indulge in these luxuries.

The father was a farmer on a small scale; that is, he cultivated ten acres of poor land, out of which he extorted a living for his family, or rather a partial living. Besides this he worked for his neighbors by the day, sometimes as a farm laborer, sometimes at odd jobs of different kinds, for he was a sort of a Jack at all trades. But his income, all told, was miserably small, and required the utmost economy and good management on the part of his wife to make it equal to the necessity of a growing family of children.

Hiram Walton was a man of good natural abilities, though of not much education, and after half an hour's conversation with him one would say, unhesitatingly, that he deserved a better fate than his hand-to-hand struggle with poverty. But he was one of those men who, for some unaccountable reason, never get on in the world. They can do a great many things creditably, but do not have the knack of conquering fortune. So Hiram had always been a poor man, and probably always would be poor. He was discontented at times, and often felt the disadvantages of his lot, but he was lacking in energy and ambition, and perhaps this was the chief reason why he did not succeed better.

After breakfast Elihu Perkins, the "cow doctor," came to the door. He was an old man with iron-gray hair, and always wore steel-bowed spectacles; at least for twenty years nobody in the town could remember ever having seen him without them. It was the general opinion that he wore them during the night. Once when questioned on the subject, he laughingly said that he "couldn't see to go to sleep without his specs".

"Well, neighbor Walton, so the cow's sick?" he said, opening the outer door without ceremony.

"Yes, Elihu, she looks down in the mouth. I hope you can save her."

"I kin tell better when I've seen the critter. When you've got through breakfast, we'll go out to the barn."

"I've got through now," said Mr. Walton, whose anxiety for the cow had diminished his appetite.

"May I go, too, father?" asked Harry, rising from the table.

"Yes, if you want to."

The three went out to the small, weather-beaten building which served as a barn for the want of a better. It was small, but still large enough to contain all the crops, which Mr. Walton could raise. Probably he could have got more out of the land if he had had means to develop its resources; but it was naturally barren, and needed much more manure than he was able to spread over it.

So the yield to an acre was correspondingly small, and likely, from year to year, to grow smaller rather than larger.

They opened the small barn door, which led to the part occupied by the cow's stall. The cow was lying down, breathing with difficulty. Elihu Perkins looked at her sharply through his specs.

"What do you think of her, neighbor Perkins?" asked the owner, anxiously.

The cow doctor shifted a piece of tobacco from one cheek to the other, and looked wise.

"I think the critter's nigh her end," he said, at last.

"Is she so bad as that?"

"Pears like it. She looks like Farmer Henderson's that died a while ago. I couldn't save her."

"Save my cow, if you can. I don't know what I should do without her."

"I'll do my best, but you mustn't blame me if I can't bring her round. You see there's this about dumb critters that makes 'em harder to cure than human bein's. They can't tell their symptoms, nor how they feel; and that's why it's harder to be a cow doctor than a doctor for humans. You've got to go by the looks, and looks is deceivin'. If I could only ask the critter how she feels, and where she feels worst, I might have some guide to go by. Not but I've had my luck. There's more'n one of 'em I've saved, if I do say it myself."

"I know you can save her if anyone can, Elihu," said Mr. Walton, who appreciated the danger of the cow, and was anxious to have the doctor begin.

"Yes, I guess I know about as much about them critters as anybody," said the garrulous old man, who had a proper appreciation of his dignity and attainments as a cow doctor. "I've had as good success as anyone I know on. If I can't cure her, you may call her a gone case. Have you got any hot water in the house?"

"I'll go in and see."

"I'll go, father," said Harry.

"Well, come right back. We have no time to lose."

Harry appreciated the need of haste as well as his father, and speedily reappeared with a pail of hot water.

"That's right, Harry," said his father. "Now you'd better go into the house and do your chores, so as not to be late for school."

Harry would have liked to remain and watch the steps, which were being taken for the recovery of the cow; but he knew he had barely time to do the "chores" referred to before school, and he was far from wishing to be late there. He had an ardent thirst for learning, and, young as he was, ranked first in the district school, which he attended. I am not about to present my young hero as a marvel of learning, for he was not so. He had improved what opportunities he had enjoyed, but these were very limited. Since he was nine years of age, his schooling had been for the most part limited to eleven weeks in the year. There was a summer as well as a winter school; but in the summer he only attended irregularly, being needed to work at home. His father could not afford to hire help, and there were many ways in which Harry, though young, could help him. So it happened that Harry, though a tolerably good scholar, was deficient in many respects, on account of the limited nature of his opportunities.

He set to work at once at the chores. First he went to the woodpile and sawed and split a quantity of wood, enough to keep the kitchen stove supplied till he came home again from school in the afternoon. This duty was regularly required of him. His father never touched the saw or the ax, but placed upon Harry the general charge of the fuel department.

After sawing and splitting what he thought to be sufficient, he carried it into the house by armfuls, and piled it up near the kitchen stove. He next drew several buckets of water from the well, for it was washing day, brought up some vegetables from the cellar to boil for lunch, and then got ready for school.

BE SURE TO LISTEN TO THE
AUDIOBOOK "STORIES OF SUCCESS"
SERIES BY HORATIO ALGER,
AVAILABLE ON AUDIBLE.COM AND
ITUNES. GO TO
WWW.SUMNERBOOKS.COM.